THE
FOOD
OF
TAIWAN

For information about permission to reproduce selections from this book,
write to Permissions, Houghton Mifflin Harcourt Publishing Company,
215 Park Avenue South, New York, New York 10003.

www.hmhco.com

Library of Congress Cataloging-in-Publication Data
Erway, Cathy, author.
The food of Taiwan : recipes from the beautiful island / Cathy Erway ; photography by Pete Lee.
pages cm
Includes index.
ISBN 978-0-544-30301-0 (paper over board); 978-0-544-30330-0 (ebk)
1. Cooking, Chinese—Taiwanese style. 2. Food—Taiwan.
3. Taiwan—Description and travel. I. Title.
TX724.5.C5E76 2015
641.5951249—dc23
2014016524

Book design by Jennifer S. Muller
Printed in China
C & C 10 9 8 7 6 5 4 3 2 1

THE FOOD OF TAIWAN

Recipes from the Beautiful Island

Cathy Erway

Photography by Pete Lee

Houghton Mifflin Harcourt

Boston New York 2015

Dedicated to the proud people of Taiwan.

This book deserves the credit of many who helped make it to fruition. I would like to thank my editor Justin Schwartz for seeing the value in a Taiwanese cookbook after so many did not, and my agent Ethan Bassoff for his longstanding enthusiasm for the project. Also, thanks to Cynthia Brzostowski and Jacqueline Beach at Houghton Mifflin Harcourt for handling its every stage of production with care.

I can't thank enough my photographer, videographer, translator, travel buddy, and friend Pete Lee for his talents in the above respects. His incredible efforts on everything from framing the perfect photo to finding people and chefs to hang out with was invaluable to this cookbook.

On that note, I'd like to thank Tina, Simon and Zoe Ma, Joy Chang, Xiao WanZi, Mr. Jian, Pete's family, Leah Huang, Cerbrina Chou, Chi-Chieh Yen, Kannie and Pea Chen, Xiao ShouShou, JenPei Aiee, and many other helpful friends along the way in my journeys in Taiwan.

I would like to thank Michael Harlan Turkell for styling many of the food shots and Norah Hoover for assisting the food photo shoot.

Special thanks to all the friends who attended my recipe-testing dinners: Tom and Katrin Helmick, Karol Lu, Dave Klopfenstein, Jordan and Ben Ho, Laena McCarthy, Leiti Hsu, Terry Seal, Rachel Wharton, John Taggart, Pervais Shallwani, Katherine Goldstein, Travis Morrison, Kara Masi, Melissa Sands, Lacey Tauber, Noah Berland, Stephanie Berland, Ali Seitz, Esther Young, Donny Tsang, James Boo, Mary Izett, Chris Cuzme, Noah Arenstein, Justin DeSpirito, Nick Gray, Josh and Rasha Kaplan, Lukas Volger, Jon Meyer, Mary Meyer, Aaron Fox, Wen-Jay Ying, Finn Smith, Erik Michielson, Debbie Kim, Andrew Gottlieb, and Jennie Gustafson.

Most importantly, thanks to my mother, Tina Chen Erway, for her help with everything from scrubbing dishes at these dinners in Brooklyn to accompanying me to her old stomping grounds in Taipei. Her interest in the foods of her homeland was an inspiration. Many thanks to my uncle, John Chen, my father, Chip Erway, and brother, Chris Erway, for their guidance and translating help, too. This book is especially dedicated to my grandparents, or Gong Gong and Po Po, for all the fearlessness and righteousness with which they embarked upon a new life in Taiwan as young adults. This spirit, I believe, very much lives on in Taiwan.

At the coast of Yeliou

Contents

5   **Acknowledgments**

8   **Foreword**

11   **Introduction**

21   The History of Taiwan

27   The People of Taiwan

33   The Land, Climate, and Agriculture of Taiwan

41   The Taiwanese Pantry

51   **Sauces and Condiments**

65   **Appetizers and Street Snacks**

97   **Vegetables**

127   **Noodles and Soups**

167   **Meat and Poultry**

199   **Seafood**

229   **Desserts and Drinks**

250   **Index**

The fish faces scared me. I was a five-year-old straight out of the supermarket suburbs of Tennessee, where all the seafood remained faceless fillets behind thick sanitized glass. At the bustling outdoor markets of Taipei, not only were the fish laid out in the open, they still had their little features intact. And, I could swear, those glassy eyeballs were looking at me.

That's probably my earliest food-related memory of Taiwan. I have since come to love the vibrant food markets that line alleys and streets throughout the country. They're noisy, messy, cramped, lush, colorful, and everything wonderful all at once. Just like Taiwan.

With this book, Cathy brings into sharp focus the wild array of flavors that define Taiwan. She explains how the country's cuisine has been shaped by its people and the history of the region. Perhaps most importantly, *The Food of Taiwan* has made all of that available and understandable to those who might be confined to shopping in the aisles of American supermarkets. Taiwanese cuisine has plenty to offer—from savory oyster omelets to delicate cake-like pineapple tarts—and this book helps ensure that all that bounty isn't confined to one small island.

Cathy took on a formidable task by writing this book. After all, Taiwanese people are obsessed with food. I realize that's an assertion that could be made about people from any number of countries, so let me offer up some solid evidence.

In the National Palace Museum outside of downtown Taipei, you can find two of the nation's treasures: One is a seven-inch tall piece of jade that's been carved into the shape of bok choy cabbage. The color of the stone perfectly mimics the white and green of real bok choy. Nearby, you'll find a brown rock set behind security glass. Why do the Taiwanese love this small, ugly stone? Because it looks like an incredibly lifelike piece of pork fat that's been cooked in soy sauce.

Even describing these artifacts as "Taiwanese" is complicated, though. The pieces were brought to the country from China by Chiang Kai-Shek in 1947, when his Kuomingtang troops were driven to Taiwan by Mao Zedong's communist party. So while they're beloved treasures revered by Taiwanese people, they're not exactly Taiwanese.

The issue of national identity in Taiwan is oftentimes fraught with caveats. When people ask about my East Asian background, the shortest, most accurate answer I can give is, "My parents are from Taiwan."

My father is Taiwanese. My mother was born in Taiwan, but her parents were from Fujian. That means I'm not exactly Taiwanese or Chinese. These are distinctions that people from Taiwan continue to make to this day. While explaining all of that is cumbersome, the awareness of those caveats means that for many, even those of us who never grew up in the country, history is always close at hand.

Through her family's story and the sections on the politics and history of Taiwan, Cathy thoughtfully and skillfully captures that complex national identity.

In this book, she writes that, as a child, her mother used to chase after a stinky tofu cart like so many American children who have trotted after a tinkling ice cream truck. Many may find it hard to believe that Taiwanese people love this odoriferously offensive food, but it's true.

Here's an example from my most recent trip back to Taiwan. While walking down the streets of Taipei with my family, every so often, we would lose my father. I'd turn around to see him standing fifty feet back, peering intently down a random alleyway. The guy had literally been stopped in his tracks by the seductive stench of stinky tofu. I kid you not.

In the section on military villages (juan cun), Cathy explains that wheat only became popular after the mainland Chinese moved to Taiwan in the late 1940s. My mother, who was born in 1952 and spent her early childhood in a rural mountain village, even now traces her love for Taiwanese-style soft white bread to the fact that bread was a treat growing up. She only got to have it when she was in the city on special occasions. When I think about Taiwan, I'm flooded with memories of my family that are invariably tied to food. There was always fresh tropical fruit available at my grandparents' house—lychees, starfruit, papaya, and crisp wax apples (lian wu). On a recent road trip to the hot springs in the north, my cousin stopped at a 7-Eleven for a snack of fish balls marinated in soy sauce, also known as the lu wei that Cathy describes. Steamy, oppressively hot summers in Taiwan meant mountains of shaved ice topped with sweet red beans, grass jelly, and taro root.

In *The Food of Taiwan*, Cathy has captured the flavors of one small island that is bursting with heart. It's a sincerely admirable feat. By sharing all of that with you, she has tapped into a true sense of Taiwanese hospitality. That's the most lasting achievement of all.

—Joy Y. Wang, food writer and journalist.

Introduction

The Presidential Office Building of Taipei is a broad, elegant building with a stately tower and Corinthian pillars. Built during Japanese rule, it faces east to meet the rising sun, before a long esplanade and the beginning of a multilane avenue. But on March 22, 2004, that stretch of pavement and much of the road behind it was swarming with protestors.

Two days before, President Chen Shui-bian of the Democratic Progressive Party was elected to his second term in office. A day before that, he was waving to supporters in a cavalcade when a bullet grazed him. He won the election, held in the frenzied aftermath of the incident, with a margin of .2 percent of the vote. Now the losing party, the Kuomintang, was holding an impassioned "sit-in" at the Presidential Building, refusing to leave even through rain and nights.

Men and women draped in plastic ponchos yelled and pumped fists as a speaker on a microphone led them. I squirmed through the crowds to get a better look at the stage that had been erected before the palace, grasping at my friends' hands just ahead. There was a line that snaked into the audience from the stage, where people were waiting their turn on the mic. Folding chairs and blankets all across the pavement reaffirmed the voices urging people to camp out overnight. Many had the night before. As I finally walked up to my group of fellow students, I was distracted by a protest organizer handing out a very important ration. With a white-gloved hand and a mask covering her face, she shoved a dome-shaped bun into my hand and moved right past me, doling them out to everyone else in sight. The familiar warm cabbagey smell of homemade dumplings wafted to my nostrils. I held the morsel—a basic shui jian bao, crisped on the bottom from a hot, oil-slicked pan, and steamed through to the swirled pinch at the top. How good could protest-rally food really be? I took a bite through the soft, delicate skin. Still warm, it burst with savory pork juice accented with white pepper and scallion. Of course it was good—this was Taiwan.

I was studying abroad at a university in Taipei that spring. My friends and I were just onlookers that day, curious about what was taking place in the city. We'd taken the subway to the city center from our college's neighborhood of Muzha in Taipei, after classes. We

At Tainan's historic Confucius Temple

didn't have any strong political beliefs, but I was becoming more aware of a rising political tension, underscored by a growing national identity and sense of Taiwanese pride during my short spring semester.

Taiwan had never been a home to me before then, but it's where my mother was born and raised before moving to the States in her twenties. My parents had met in Taiwan in the 1970s, when my dad took a job with an import-export company based in Taipei. As a recent grad from Cornell who majored in Asian studies, my father spoke Chinese and could advise the company on Western customs, like what Santa Claus wears. My mother worked for the company, too; they met on my father's first day on the job. After marrying, my parents eventually settled in New Jersey, after living at times in San Francisco and New York City. I never planned on spending a semester of college in Taiwan— and neither did anyone in my family. But when the opportunity to apply for a teach-study scholarship program in Taipei suddenly presented itself during my senior year of college, I just knew that I had to sign up. It would be for my last semester of college, but why not? There was no question about it; I just had to go.

The world of Taiwan—and especially its food—became three-dimensional to me almost from the moment I stepped off the plane. Suddenly, all the foods that I had grown up eating made so much sense to me. All the aromas and tastes were so much richer. And they were so varied! While I could recall my mother making stir-fries with slivered pork and vegetables as a go-to dinner routine at home, in Taiwan I got to taste the tender, gelatinous strips of pork belly and crisp, herbal Chinese celery tossed rapidly together in a smoking-hot wok. The Taiwanese fried chicken, its crackly, seasoned crust served atop rice and a drizzle of sauce, was something that I'd never encountered at home. Salty, soothing eggs dyed from a warm bath of soy sauce–based broth that I snacked on frequently as a child were available everywhere in Taiwan, in

all different shades and sizes. One slurp of a beef noodle soup's broth was practically enough protein for the day, so dense and satisfying it was—yet also so reminiscent of my mother's weekend favorite red-braised beef stews. I delighted in visiting the night markets, which were all the rage among students, tasting something new around every corner: one night it might be a simple, yet beautifully prepared thick soup of fresh squid, and another, a crazy, chewy concoction with the likes of oysters and eggs folded together with a clear, starchy gel. Pretty soon I realized that I was eating fairly nonstop—and it seemed most people were as well. The sheer number of roadside restaurants, street carts, and night market vendors, and the passion with which people spoke of their favorites, indicated that Taiwan is an island obsessed with food. Good food, and all kinds of it.

Most of the experiences I had in Taiwan were punctuated by food. A trip to the coastal city of Danshui, for instance, meant tasting every local signature served by vendors along the waterfront. Breaks in between classes entailed grabbing snacks like crispy youtiao, a box of dumplings, or bento lunch and any number of iced, sweetened drinks. "Hanging out" simply meant eating, shopping, and the occasional karaoke booth session. It wasn't just eating any old thing for an exciting night out, though. It could be a half-dozen or so stands at a night market, or a new and trendy shop specializing in steak, yakitori, Sichuan food, spaghetti, or hot pot. The emphasis on food in Taiwan was perfectly fine with me. Growing up, my family treated food as the focal point of any gathering, and a definite highlight of the day. Every night we sat around the table for family meals prepared by my mother, and often on weekends, by my father. It wasn't always Chinese food, of course; my mom had learned with great enthusiasm how to cook American staples like meatloaf and barbecued chicken. For holidays, my parents would (and still do) take turns, my mother preparing an elaborate

Chinese-style meal of many courses the night before Christmas or Thanksgiving, and my father preparing the requisite turkey, or prime rib, the next. There was nothing too strange to try when it came to exploring food, either. My family's motto very much was: If it exists, then we'd like to try it. My father even kept a paper menu of his favorite Malaysian restaurant and would cross off dishes he'd tried in pencil. The next outing there, he'd place it in his pocket and unfold the menu to order only things that weren't yet crossed off. I was beginning to realize, during my college years, that not every family in the States shared our borderline obsessions with food. In Taiwan, I felt like I'd found my homeland.

My grandparents, my uncle, and aunt had all moved to the States from Taiwan during my early childhood, so there had been no reason to visit the island ever since my first trip there at the age of six. Our family lost touch with what was going on in Taiwan throughout the eighties and nineties. They missed out on experiencing firsthand many of the transformations the island underwent in the meantime: the lift of martial law in 1987; the first democratically elected president in 1996; the lift on bans for direct mail and flights between mainland China and Taiwan in 2008; and the rise of other political parties that were not solely the KMT, like the Democratic Progressive Party.

Such things would have been unfathomable at the time when my mother's parents had immigrated to Taiwan from Hunan Province in 1948—along with some two million people from throughout mainland China. This was during China's civil war, when Mao Zedong's People's Republic of China (PRC) was gaining ground, forcing Chiang Kai-shek's Republic of China (ROC) to retreat to the island. Their plan was to stay in Taiwan only temporarily, to regroup and gather the strength to take back their country. Things didn't turn out the way the ROC would have liked, and they've remained based in Taiwan ever since.

My grandparents never imagined they'd be planting their roots in Taiwan; to them it was a mere stopover, an unfortunate hiccup in the war. But had my mother and her generation been born and raised in mainland China instead of Taiwan, her life would have been a whole different story. I was just beginning to see exactly where she came from, and what aspects of her unique homeland I'd inherited from her while living in Taiwan that spring of 2004.

A Slippery "Status-Quo"

Now, we understand that the shootings that took place in March 2004 had been a sincere assassination attempt on the president by an individual acting alone. The suspect was never charged as he committed suicide before being discovered. The former president Chen Shui-bian was incarcerated after completing his second term on charges of embezzlement, however. Currently, the reigning president of Taiwan is the Kuomintang (KMT) leader Ma Ying-jeou, who has garnered controversy for appearing to be more cooperative with Beijing than former Taiwanese leaders. No one could have predicted all these things those impassioned days just after the election in 2004. Still, the protest was somewhat misguided; most of the people I spoke with at the sit-in and the days after in Taipei were upset because they thought the shootings were an elaborate hoax the president had staged in order to turn the election with sympathy votes. A long, flowing banner hanging onstage at the presidential palace rallies had read, "We want truth. We want justice." Perhaps it goes much deeper than that. These protestors' opposition to the president was rooted in a decades-old clash. On that same day, in the southern Taiwan city of Tainan, supporters of the Democratic Progressive Party were celebrating the reelection as a momentous sign of victory for the Taiwanese who had been on the island for generations, of which Chen was one. But in the KMT's home base of

My brother and me at Chiang Kai-Shek Memorial Hall, 1988 / My brother and me at Sun Moon Lake, 1988

Taipei, its supporters were just not willing to swallow the notion of not being the true leaders of Taiwan. And until just a few decades ago, they weren't even willing to accept not being the true government of China. For their part, the Democratic Progressive Party's message hinged on empowering the "true" Taiwanese people, who were oppressed by the various groups who ruled over them during the last two centuries. Although largely criticized for appealing to this angle without solid policy to back it up, the DPP and Chen have indeed invigorated a sense of Taiwanese identity and pride. Their call for independence has waxed and waned periodically throughout the last three decades in Taiwan—increasing tensions with the mainland that have at times prompted shows of military strength. "But as it stands, China still claims Taiwan is its territory, even though Taiwan is self-governed outside of Beijing rule."

Indeed, I had stumbled upon Taiwan at a visceral stage of its identity crisis. And as far as we know, there had never really been a time on the island without one.

The Sunflower Student Movement

Ten years after the reelection of President Chen Shui-bian and the Taipei "sit-ins" afterward, Taiwan was embroiled in another passionate debate. In the spring of 2014, the Presidential Office Building was again teeming with protestors—this time, of a younger, college-age population, and they were singing a drastically different tune. Holding sunflowers as a sign of hope and occupying the presidential palace and its surrounding streets, these students were protesting a controversial trade deal between China and the ROC, called the Cross-Strait Service Trade Agreement. This "sit-in" lasted from March 18 to roughly April 10, after several rounds of negotiations between the ruling-party KMT and the DPP. The Democratic

Progressive Party was aligned with the student rebellion's concerns, which was that closer trade ties with China would make it more vulnerable toward political pressures from its neighbor. After weeks of negotiations during the occupation, an agreement was not reached, leaving the KMT to pursue its economic relationship with China. But in the months afterward, the Sunflower Movement was successful in reanimating an international conversation on the broader theme of Taiwan's economic independence as a means of protecting its political independence from Beijing. This sentiment was expressed by Hillary Clinton in June 2014, in a statement she made to *Business Weekly* magazine. A wariness of China's political oversight was also felt by the students and people of Hong Kong in the fall of 2014, who launched an occupation protesting elected leaders being vetted by Beijing, a protest that some speculate was inspired by Taiwan's.

Is China Taiwan's founding father or ultimate foe? A bullish presence and insult to Democratic agendas, or a great economic opportunity and cultural kin? Who am I to say? But some 100,000 protestors came out to these demonstrations in 2014, and although I was not there to witness them this time, much of the world took notice. Its significance cannot be underestimated for the future of the island.

The Birth of a Cuisine

There is something exciting about a culture that is just coming into its own. Politics aside, the idea of Taiwan as having a distinct and unified culture is a thesis that has been gaining support in recent years. Along with that, that Taiwan has a unified and distinct cuisine in and of itself; a cuisine that would have never been without the waves of migration and war, yet holds its own legacy.

Goats graze at a countryside farm

One hallmark of national pride might just be its beef noodle soup, for instance. The dish bears resemblances to mainland Chinese cooking, yet is a treasured specialty of Taiwan. Another is Koxinga, the Ming Dynasty hero who formed the first independent state on Taiwan (who we'll hear about later on in the History section). The diverse melting pot that makes up Taiwan's population is also celebrated on the island as a point of distinction. While its national language is Mandarin, for train announcements in Taiwan, you'll hear messages in Mandarin followed by repeats in Hokkien (the southern Taiwanese or "Taiwanese" dialect, rooted in Fujian province); Hakka (a traditionally oppressed and dispersed Chinese minority group, which Taiwan has significant populations of); and often a Taiwanese aboriginal dialect, depending on where you're located. I have observed a burgeoning interest in traditional art and folk music from the fishermen, farmers, and tea pickers of Taiwan. Also, there is a surge of interest in preserving the cultures of the aboriginal tribes in Taiwan, with television stations devoted to this community and pop stars proudly claiming this heritage. This might seem almost contradictory to the open-armed stance that Taiwan places itself in the modern first world. The Taiwanese are quick to embrace the latest trends in popular culture from Western countries, South Korea, and Japan. Taiwan is eager to welcome tourists from around the world, to learn English, and to send its best students overseas. It is keen to import English-speaking students and teachers, if my academic sojourn in Taipei is any proof. And it has had a thoroughly democratic government since 1996.

Yet amid all the rage over international fashion, music celebrities, or the latest culinary import, there is a conspicuous interest in traditional Taiwanese cuisine. This is seen in restaurants such as Shin Yeh and Chingye Shinleyuan in Taiwan, which were both founded by female restauranteurs and have become legendary for their sophistication in old-fashioned Taiwanese cooking. It is also demonstrated in the popular BaoHaus bun shop in New York, where its outspoken Taiwanese-American chef Eddie Huang has popularized the Taiwanese brand of pork belly buns. Taiwanese cuisine has been explored in a book by Chen Jingyi, a Taiwanese writer who shined a spotlight on the history of famous dishes found throughout the island in loving detail. And also by Jade and Muriel Chen in Australia, restauranteurs who have published a cookbook that illuminates their unique culinary homeland. There have always been regional specialties throughout Taiwan, which are fiercely prided by locals and sought out by domestic travelers. But today, there is a growing chorus of thought on uniquely Taiwanese food as a whole.

What exactly is traditional Taiwanese cuisine? Like any place or peoples, it is rooted in humble peasant dishes. This bedrock gives itself away with the use of dried or fermented ingredients, or with offal cuts of meat, and homely, rough vegetables. It shows its slip whenever a dish so seemingly crude and inexpensive has become a source of immense pride and fondness, appearing even on banquet tables. It evolves when these beloved comfort dishes of a country are refined over time, improved upon and expanded in myriad ways by adoring cooks along the way. This is certainly the case for Taiwan's favorite traditional foods, and it's happening all the time and in different stages with newer beloved dishes.

When I set out to write a cookbook on the food of Taiwan, I had to keep asking myself, what makes this dish distinctly Taiwanese? Meaning, not something that's merely a riff or extension of something that you'd find in some part of mainland China, nor an attempt at something from an even more far-flung locale (sorry, but Taiwanese pizza is not quite it). One way of looking at how a cuisine is created is to examine the social factors that led to its formation: the military camps where families from all over

China mingled and cooked their meals and the small food businesses that cropped up around temples in Tainan, serving worshippers as they came and went. Geography and lifestyle figure heavily into this as well, with the influences of the coastal regions' easy catches and the nine-to-five hustle-bustle of the average, largely middle-class workday. We will look at the social and recreational habits of modern-day Taiwanese, like night markets, to see where the cuisine might be evolving. Throughout the recipes, we'll explore the quick meals served for commuters on the go and the ever-popular night market culture, where young people rush to the trendiest stalls. We'll also take a closer look at the preferences in ingredients and texture concerning Taiwanese food today. Also, we'll explore the ways in which overseas influences have found their way into food culture as part of the larger popular culture.

Upon deciding to write a cookbook on the food of Taiwan, I hoped that this would only be the beginning of a larger dialogue. I don't attempt to know every

My grandparents and my mother, Taipei, circa 1951

intricacy nor history nor regional specialty, but to invite those conversations for the long run. It is an endless and ever expanding topic anyway, with new dimensions being built onto it as we speak. I also acknowledge that as an American-born, half-Taiwanese writer, this is absolutely not an exhaustive study nor the most intimate. But I will say that when deciding to write this book, it really comes down to this picture.

The proud, hopeful faces of my grandparents holding my infant mother are profound to me. I will never forget the courage and audacity that my forebears demonstrated when they decided to move away from their families to a strange island, in which their future was unknown.

There's a saying in Taiwan that one is a "taro root" if they're from Taiwan (because the shape of the root vegetable resembles the island's shape), or they're a "sweet potato leaf" if from mainland China (before the conquest of Manchuria, for shape reasons again). My grandparents would then be a sweet potato leaf in this equation. But no coincidence, these are food–based metaphors, and taro roots and sweet potato leaves are common items at the Taiwanese table. For reasons of universalizing this cuisine, I have focused largely on dishes that can be translated easily using similar ingredients found in America or focusing on those using ingredients that are already eaten and readily found here in the average grocery market. Locally-grown substitutions and adjustments are not a huge concern to me, having grown up with my mother's cooking. In fact, substituting ingredients—with what is locally available—is emblematic of the many peoples who settled in Taiwan, as evidenced in the recipes throughout this book. Even still, tasty food traditions hold their own. When blended with environmental factors and cultural influences, something magical happens. This is exactly what I believe has happened with Taiwanese cuisine as a whole.

The History of Taiwan

Taiwan has been inhabited by various aboriginal tribes for thousands of years. Yet only a hundred miles off the eastern coast of China, little was recorded about Taiwan and its inhabitants by even the Chinese empire until the modern era.

In 1544, a Portuguese ship passing by Taiwan named it Ilha Formosa, or Beautiful Island. Shortly afterward, the Spanish landed and found Taiwan to be a rich source of sulfur, an element in gunpowder. The Dutch arrived and established the Dutch East India Company outpost on Taiwan in 1624, trading sugar, spices, and silk. Their colony increased due to the profitable trade, and the Dutch built two forts, one in the north and the south of the island by the mid-1600s.

At this time in mainland China, the Ming Dynasty was overthrown by Manchurians, resulting in the Qing

Chiang Kai-Shek Memorial in Taipei

The gardens of the historic Confucius Temple of Tainan /
A statue of the Ming leader Koxinga in Tainan

Dynasty. However, a leader of the Ming loyalists known as Koxinga (or Zheng Chenggong) carried on valiant efforts to oust the new dynasty and revive Ming rule. Koxinga and his troops were forced farther south by their opponents and in 1660 they decided to regroup on the island of Taiwan.

Koxinga is revered as a hero in Taiwan, and is even thought of as a founding father (especially in the south, where Tainan served as its first capital). The military leader had an unusual background: the son of a Chinese merchant and a Japanese woman, he was born and raised until the age of seven in Japan (a fact that the Japanese who would later colonize Taiwan would call attention to). Koxinga led many successful campaigns for the ultimately failing Ming dynasty, but the greatest achievement for which he is remembered is defeating Dutch rule on Taiwan. This was achieved in the Siege of Fort Zeelandia on the southwest coast of Taiwan in 1662, effectively forcing the Dutch out and gaining control of the island. However, Koxinga did not enjoy his victory long and died of malaria in the same year. His son continued the independent kingdom they established on Taiwan until he was defeated by the Qing Dynasty in 1683.

Afterward, more mainland Chinese began trickling over to Taiwan, mining for sulfur and other resources, but it was seen as dangerous terrain—rife with diseases and head-hunting aborigines. For these reasons, it didn't attract much foreign interest until the end of the 1800s, when China lost the first Sino-Japanese War and ceded Taiwan to the Japanese empire. From 1895 to 1945, Japan occupied Taiwan.

Things got off to a very rough start between the existing communities on Taiwan and its Japanese rulers. Determined to make its sovereign territory profitable and extract its resources, the Japanese led ruthless campaigns against the aborigines, who receded to the mountains. They stamped out a short-lived resistance by the Taiwanese of Chinese heritage on the island. They built railroads and established the first education system on the island (its sovereign pupils would read, write, and learn in Japanese). They performed extensive scientific research to alleviate the risk of infectious disease. For much of the second half of the Japanese period, Taiwan was fairly peaceful. Older generations in Taiwan remember the period from their childhood as relatively good times, even, for the island. At least, in comparison with what happened next.

After the bombing of Hiroshima in 1945, Japan surrendered to the Allies, effectively ceding all its foreign colonies. Critically, however, they did not specify exactly whom they were ceding Taiwan to. And by then, the Qing Dynasty was no more. It had been overthrown by China's first modern democracy in 1912, the Republic of China (ROC), led by Sun Yat-sen. But China remained in grip of civil war for decades afterward. After Sun died in 1925, Chiang Kai-shek of the Chinese Nationalist Party, or the Kuomintang, was appointed his successor. Sun believed in containing the disparate factions under the flag of the ROC, despite mounting tensions with Chinese Communists, or the People's Republic of China (PRC). Chiang, however, wanted to defeat the Communists. By the late 1940s, the PRC, led by Mao Zedong, were forcing the Nationalists farther south, into Sichuan province. Chiang and his government sought temporary refuge on the island of Taiwan.

When the Kuomintang arrived in Taiwan in 1947, they did not tread lightly. The KMT military leader who led this mission, Chen Yi, persecuted thousands of innocent people who resisted the invasion. The incident, which began on February 28, 1947, is known today as the 2-2-8 massacre. Chiang Kai-shek, his entire army and its dependents, and many supporters of the ROC constituting 1.5 to 2 million people in total, moved from the mainland to Taiwan from 1948–1949. Martial law was declared on the island.

Initially, the Republic of China was recognized internationally as the true government of China, in exile on Taiwan. As the decades passed and they were still unable to challenge the Communists on the mainland, this attitude changed. The ROC lost its seat in the UN to the PRC in 1971. In 1972, President Nixon visited Beijing, a gesture that was viewed as acknowledging the PRC's legitimacy as China's government. Meanwhile, on Taiwan the KMT government implemented a land reform program that is viewed by experts as a great success. As farmers enjoyed better security, industries grew, the middle class flourished, and the island enjoyed greater prosperity through the 1960s and 70s. Chiang Kai-shek's son succeeded his father in 1975 and continued single-party rule, although he lifted martial law in 1987. Before his death in 1988, he appointed Lee Teng-hui as the next president of the ROC. Lee was the first Taiwan-born president and a skilled, Japanese-educated economist. He led the island through an economic boom, fueled by Taiwan's high-tech industry. Lee established greater democracy throughout his presidency, allowing new political parties to be formed, and dismantling superfluous branches of the government designed by the KMT under the assumption that it ruled China.

In 1996, Lee won reelection in the island's first true presidential elections. Since then, economic growth has been slower on the island, but it has established a national health insurance system, social welfare programs, and has made progress in educational standards. Today, 95 percent of Taiwanese students complete high school and go on to trade school or college. The Taipei World Financial Center, or Taipei 101, was built in 2004 and for five years enjoyed the status of the world's tallest building. In 2000, Chen Shui-bian of the Democratic Progressive Party won Taiwan's second democratic election. Ma Ying-jeou of the Kuomintang won election in 2008, and serves as Taiwan's current president.

A tea farmer in Maokong, which overlooks Taipei / A view of Taipei from the mountains

From left: Folk signer Ha Wan and Chef Chen Yao-Zhong, both of the Amis tribe / Children walking home from school / Young drummers of the Paiwan tribe in traditional dress

The People of Taiwan

Taiwan's diverse population is greatly prided on the island. A land of 23.3 million, its people can be divided roughly into four major groups, although intermarriage makes it impossible to designate exact numbers to each. A majority of Taiwanese are of Hoklo descent, originally from Fujian Province in China. These are descendants of people who immigrated across the Taiwan Strait before the Japanese takeover in 1895. Their populations are most prominent in the southern counties of Taiwan, where Taiwan's capital was situated before the northern city of Taipei was named its capital as a state under the Qing Dynasty in 1886.

The mainland Chinese people who settled in Taiwan in the late 1940s were a varied group. In addition to soldiers and their families, about a million civilians traveled along with the ROC from all throughout China. Many of them were scholars, musicians, Buddhist monks, businessmen—people who were wary of the Communist regime. These also included China's minority groups such as Muslims and Mongolians.

Taiwan's aboriginal tribes account for 2 percent of its population, roughly half a million people, and are divided among fourteen officially recognized tribes.

A family meal served at home

From top left: A Buddhist monk amidst the crowd / Vendors chatting in an alley before business hours / A cosmopolitan strip in the city of Kaoshiung

There are numerous unrecognized tribes, as well as efforts to preserve their languages and culture on the island. Many distinct tribes in Taiwan became extinct or were assimilated into other tribes over the years due to war and oppression. Anthropologists have categorized Taiwan's aboriginals as Austronesian peoples, an ethnic group of Southeast Asia and Oceania found in regions as far-flung as Madagascar and Hawaii. They are also the majority ethnic group of Malaysia and the Philippines. As such, they are not of China's majority ethnic group, Han Chinese.

The Hakka people are dispersed throughout China and the world, and constitute another large group on Taiwan. The Hakka began settling in Taiwan in the 1800s to escape oppression on the mainland. Once thought to be a distinct ethnicity, the Hakka are now widely recognized as Han Chinese, yet they have their own language and customs. The Hakka are known as a hardworking people, establishing agricultural communities in less desirable areas of Taiwan. A wonderful cookbook of the rustic cuisine of the Hakka diaspora was published in 2012 by Linda Lau Anusasananan.

Taiwan's legacy as a haven for the oppressed or the opportunistic continues. There have been recent waves of migration from Southeast Asian countries, many of them women seeking domestic work. Businessmen and expats from other foreign countries comprise about 5 percent of Taiwan's current residents.

Despite these foreign migrations, Taiwan's population is projected to decrease. Following a postwar birth boom in the 1950s and 60s, Taiwan's birth rate has gradually declined. It dropped below the replacement level (needed to replace the current population) in the 1980s, and in 2010, Taiwan held the lowest birth rate in the world. Many have speculated the shrinking numbers are attributed to education, overseas travel, relocation, and a career-focused female population.

A fun restaurant outing / Cooks tools / Shopping for groceries in a day market

The Land, Climate, and Agriculture of Taiwan

An island of 35,883 square kilometers, Taiwan sits just off the eastern coast of China, to the south of the Japanese archipelago, and to the north of the Philippines. It has a subtropical climate, spanning the Tropic of Cancer. More than 50 percent of Taiwan is covered with wooded forest and jungle. Its east is mostly mountainous, with five mountain ranges running alongside the eastern coast. The lowlands of Taiwan's west and north are populated rather evenly, with cities alongside the west from north to south. The Penghu Islands, or the Pescadores, lie to the southwest and are part of Taiwan. Taiwan experiences rainy seasons in the winter and a summer monsoon, and has an overall hot, humid climate. Among Taiwan's unique natural resources are its hot springs. Thanks to a tectonic plate collision zone underneath, warm, clear water swells from four major locations in Taiwan and are enjoyed as spas. Taiwan is prone to earthquakes and typhoons due to its unique geography, as well.

Eroded rock formations on the coast at Yeliou

From top: A rocky northern beach / Hot springs swell from the mountains

Taiwan is home to incredible natural landscapes, from lush mountains to fantastic coastal rock formations. There are eight government-protected national parks throughout Taiwan, and thirteen national scenic areas (the latter promoted by the tourism bureau). These reserves are home to diverse wildlife and fauna, and often aboriginal communities. Major destinations for visitors include natural spectacles like Taroko Gorge and Sun Moon Lake, the mountain range Yangminshan, and the coral reefs of Kenting.

Taiwan is well suited for growing sugarcane and rice. These industries had been established on the island as early as the Dutch rule, and continued to be important agricultural exports. Specialty crops like tropical fruits and high-mountain teas are major exports today as well. Taiwan is world renowned for producing some of the most distinctive tea, grown in its mountainous terrain. With only one-quarter of its land suitable for agriculture, however, and with slowing domestic demand due to joining the WTO in 2001, Taiwan's farmland has been gradually decreasing.

Surrounded by coasts, Taiwan has a well-established fishing industry. Coastal regions are predominantly fishing communities, supplying the island's massive appetite for all manners of seafood. One can spot a temple dedicated to the Taoist goddess of the sea—the fishermen's god—poking from the hilltops in most of the coastal towns and cities throughout Taiwan. Fishing boats and aquaculture beds for seafood like oysters or shrimp are common sights in these places, too. Interestingly, Taiwan's fishing legacy has become a nostalgic sport as well, with the rise of recreational aquaculture facilities where clientele can pay to fish from pools and cook up their "catch" at home.

From top: Farmers looking over a bridge / A rooftop home vegetable patch / A field of rice paddies

A lush farm in Ilan county

From top left: Boathouses on Sun Moon Lake / Water buffalo at a farm in Ilan county / A thick forest in Sitou / A view from the mountains

The relatively small scale of its agricultural production reduces Taiwan's ability to compete in international markets. Taiwan raises much of its own livestock (for pork, chicken, and beef), but in response to an increasing demand, imports much meat as well. There is little in the way of wild game except in aboriginal communities. These aboriginal communities have preserved their customs of producing millet-based products and foraging wild mountain vegetables much more effectively than hunting game, however. In aboriginal villages, one can taste millet-based wines and mochi, and a variety of wild greens such as dragon's beard fern (page 112). The latter plant has even become popular among nonaboriginal Taiwanese as a delicacy, trucked in by aboriginal farmers to produce markets.

The Taiwanese are proud of their domestically produced goods, especially where food is concerned. Wary of PRC health regulations (or lack thereof), food products made in Taiwan are much favored by average households, and there is growing demand for organic and non-GMO food in Taiwan. In 2013, Taiwan announced its plans to triple organic farming by 2020, to boost the economy and satisfy this demand.

From top: Paddle boarders on the beach / A driftwood-strewn beach / Sun Moon Lake

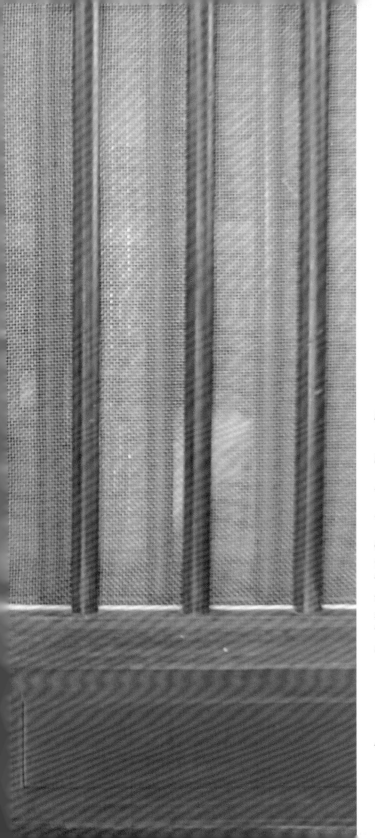

The Taiwanese Pantry

One can find all the ingredients for the recipes in this book in a well-stocked Asian supermarket. The Taiwanese pantry is not exorbitant: one need not stock up on numerous dried spices, pastes, and herbs. Here are some of the most common ingredients used in Taiwanese cooking. In the first recipe chapter, Sauces and Condiments, we will provide recipes for a few more.

An old-fashioned cabinet

From top left: Freshly made rice noodles / Patrons lining up for a food cart / A street vendor selling soup dumplings / Dried shrimp / A dried seafood vendor at a daytime outdoor food market

Chili bean sauce

A signature condiment of Sichuan province, this sauce marries fermented beans and chilies in a pungent, pastelike mixture. Numerous variations exist: some may be studded with black soy beans while others, with yellow-colored fava beans, may be whole or mostly mashed up. Fermented bean sauce with or without the addition of chilies is also used in Taiwan; on page 154 we'll use a sweet, nonspicy fermented bean sauce called tienmianjiang to make zha jiang mian noodles (page 154). However, chili bean sauce is easiest to find in groceries in the U.S., and is widely used in Taiwanese cooking.

Cilantro

This distinctive herb is used liberally throughout Taiwan. Chopped—both stems and leaves, typically—it's a ubiquitous garnish for soups, stir-fries and rice plates, adding a floral touch and color.

Cornstarch

Used to add clear, thick body to soups and sauces as well as to marinate meats and seafood, cornstarch is key in many Taiwanese recipes. Traditionally, the Taiwanese would use regular potato or arrowroot starch for these same purposes, but the common cornstarch found in the U.S. achieves the desired effects in these recipes, except where noted.

Crushed peanut powder

Like fried shallots (see page 52), crushed peanuts are a savory, crunchy topping often used in Taiwan. Typically, the peanuts are ground to a finer consistency than one can achieve by simply chopping the nuts by hand, and they're blended with sugar. This topping is seen in the Taiwanese steamed pork belly bun or gua bao (page 67), but it can also be sprinkled atop stir-fried dishes or sautéed vegetables for contrast.

Dried baby shrimp

These little nuggets are full of briny umami flavor and are used, often soaked and minced, to flavor a wide variety of foods in Taiwan. They store well in an airtight container in the refrigerator, making them an easy option for a little extra flavor in a sautéed vegetable dish, for example.

Dried rice noodles

Taiwanese rice noodles are thin and delicate, unlike the flat, broad noodles of Thai dishes like pad thai. Rice is a staple crop of Taiwan, requiring much warmer climates than wheat, and this was the main type of noodles found on the island for centuries.

Dried shiitake mushrooms

Another common ingredient that packs a lot of flavor per portion. These dried mushrooms are best soaked for at least 30 minutes in cold or room-temperature water until spongy and fully reconstituted. Their resulting soaking water can be added to soups or used to flavor stir-fries.

Dried wheat noodles

With the influence of mainland Chinese cuisines, wheat noodles have become popular in Taiwan, too. These may come in any variety of shapes and sizes, for any preference. One can also find fresh, hand-pulled wheat noodles from specialty shops and restaurants in Taiwan.

Fermented black beans

Salty and pungent, these whole beans are actually soy beans that have been fermented—not to be confused with the common black turtle bean. They are used throughout Chinese cuisines, and are related to soy sauce (which is brewed from fermented soy beans). Just a small pinch may be added to flavor stir-fries and braised dishes. If difficult to find, a dab of fermented black bean sauce—often found in jars as "black bean garlic sauce"—may be substituted.

Five-spice powder

A quintessential ingredient in red-braised stews, this is a ground spice blend of star anise, fennel seed, cinnamon, cloves, and Sichuan peppercorns, although variations and additional spices may occur.

Fresh chili sauce

Crushed, bright red chilies macerated in vinegar and salt, often with chopped garlic added, is an everyday condiment found in Taiwan. It can be added to the plate for dipping dumplings or buns, or used to add a touch of heat to stir-fries while cooking in the pan.

Fresh chilies

Vibrant red chilies are used sparingly in Taiwanese cooking to add color and just a touch of heat. Commonly, these are large, finger-shaped bird's eye, or Thai chilies, which have softened in heat level due to their ripe, red color.

Fresh Thai basil

Fragrant basil leaves are tossed in at the last moment to stir-fries in many famous Taiwanese dishes (like Three Cup Chicken, see page 169). This basil variety has slightly serrated, spiky leaves and a somewhat more intense anise flavor than Italian basil, but in a pinch, Italian basil will do just fine for these recipes as a substitute.

Ginger

Fresh ginger root is a ubiquitous ingredient in Taiwanese cooking. The Taiwanese distinguish between "old" ginger root (with a rough, tan skin and fibrous interior) and "young" ginger, which is pearly pink and virtually skinless, with a crisp interior and milder taste. Young ginger is used mostly as a delicate garnish, whereas old ginger is more potent and often sliced up for stews and stir-fries. We will be referring to "old" ginger whenever ginger is mentioned in this book.

"Gourmet powder"

Most Taiwanese households have a small canister of this flavor enhancer, which is mostly MSG with white pepper and salt, and sometimes other spices added. However, I don't call for this ingredient in any of the recipes in this book, opting for a combination of salt and white pepper or other spices as needed.

Ma-la chili oil

Dried chili peppers are crushed and cooked in oil with Sichuan peppercorns to make this unique condiment. The fusion of these ingredients create a numbing, hot sensation (ma-la) that's both tingly and spicy. This condiment was not typical in Taiwan until after the mainland arrival of the mid-1900s. Today, however, Sichuan food enjoys great popularity in Taiwan and this condiment is often found at dumpling stands along with vinegar and soy sauce.

Rice vinegar

Taiwanese food often has a tinge of tanginess from natural rice vinegar. It may be clear, or aged so that it develops a warm, brownish tint. Black vinegar, an aged variety, is often used in Taiwan, and will have slightly less acidity and a sweeter taste than clear rice vinegars.

Rice wine

Not to be confused with rice vinegar, rice wine is used most often in stews and soups, or to marinate meats and seafood. Its slightly sweet, delicate flavor adds dimension to foods and is often thought to be a perfect counterbalance for strong-tasting seafood. It is perfectly acceptable to swap in Japanese rice wine (sake) if Taiwanese or Chinese rice wine is not to be found.

From top left: Rock sugar / Thai basil and red chilies / The spices in five-spice powder / A cook at a seafood market kitchen

From top: Patrons enjoying a hot pot restaurant / Grabbing a late night street snack

Sesame oil

Used throughout East Asia, this incredibly fragrant oil is made from toasted sesame seeds. The oil ranges from light tan to deep brown in color, depending on how well the seeds were toasted. Because of its rich flavor, it's often used as a flavoring agent, such as to marinate meats, or drizzle atop dishes once they're out of the wok, instead of for cooking.

Sha-cha sauce

This wonderfully savory sauce incorporates ground dried shrimp and fish along with shallots and dried chilies in oil, with a pastelike consistency. Although most households purchase the sauce in jars, I've provided a recipe for homemade sha-cha sauce on page 53.

Soy sauce

Dark soy sauce:

Darker and more robust than light soy sauce, dark soy sauce is often used in long-simmered dishes like red-braised pork, to add more distinctive color and deeper flavor.

Light soy sauce:

Not to be confused with low-sodium or "lite" soy sauces available on the market, light soy sauce simply means regular soy sauce in this book. It is more transparent, with less body, than dark soy sauce. It's used in everything from stir-fries to quick sauces and dressings as a quintessential flavoring agent.

Thick soy sauce:

A starch-thickened, diluted, and slightly sweetened version of soy sauce, thick soy sauce is often used as a dip. Most Taiwanese homes have a bottle of it and even cook with the sauce in place of soy sauce, wherever a touch of sweetness and thickness is desired. It is similar to oyster sauce, which may be substituted.

Sugar

A touch of sugar is common throughout Taiwanese recipes. In Taiwan, most households have natural clusters of "rock sugar" for cooking purposes (sugar is after all a major crop in Taiwan). However, natural, unbleached sugar or just white sugar may be used in any of the recipes instead.

Sweet potato or yam starch

Extracted from white sweet potatoes, this powder is a secret weapon for perfecting many signature Taiwanese dishes. It's preferable over other starches to create a stiffer clear gel (like in oyster omelets) or a more crackly crust on fried foods (like fried chicken bites or oysters). It can be found in Asian supermarkets although precise labeling in English may be inconsistent; look for "sweet potato starch" or "yam starch" as it might otherwise be plain old potato starch, which won't have the same effect.

White pepper

This everyday seasoning is used to season meats, seafood, eggs, and soup broths—much like ground black pepper in the Western tradition. The Taiwanese prefer white pepper for its unique flavor and because it doesn't add dark specks to dishes, especially with light-colored foods. Sometimes, dishes call for a dusting of white pepper for garnish; canisters are commonly found at restaurant tables for this option as well.

White rice

Taiwanese rice tends to be short-grain and cooks up slightly more moist than long-grain white rice. However, long-grain or short-grain white rice are suitable for use in any of the recipes, unless noted.

Sauces
and
Condiments

Pickled Mustard Green (page 57) / Sha-Cha Sauce (page 53)

Fried Shallots
(Hong Cong Tou)

紅蔥頭

Makes about ½ cup

Crispy, golden fried shallots are a common garnish in Taiwan. Whether floating across soups or sprinkled atop rice bowls, they lend a sweet, crunchy depth to dishes. In Taiwan, one can purchase a canister of them to keep in the pantry. But if you don't mind a quick fry session at home, you can easily make a fresh batch yourself.

6 medium shallots

½ cup vegetable or peanut oil, or more as needed, for frying

Slice the shallots as thinly and as uniformly as possible (with the help of a mandolin if desired).

Add the oil to a small saucepan so that the oil is at least ½ inch deep (use more oil if necessary). Heat over medium-high until a candy thermometer inserted into the oil (but not touching the pan) reads between 350° to 375°F. Add the shallots all at once and begin stirring. Continue to cook, stirring, until most of the shallots have turned yellow-gold, about 2 minutes. Remove from the oil using a slotted spoon or tongs and transfer immediately to paper towels. Let cool for about 1 minute before using.

Use immediately or store in an airtight container for up to 1 day.

Sha-Cha Sauce (Sha Cha Jiang)

沙茶醬

Makes about 1 cup

This classic condiment in Taiwan is often labeled "barbecue sauce" in English. That's because it shares the same root name as satay sauce in Southeast Asian cuisines. However, sha-cha sauce does not resemble the common, peanutty interpretations of satay sauce today: it's a minced paste of dried fish and shrimp, shallots, garlic, and chilies. It actually shares more similarities with the Hong Kong "XO sauce" in its ingredient composition. The sauce is sometimes used as a marinade that is brushed on before food hits the grill—see the grilled corn recipe on page 88. However, it's more commonly used in Taiwan to flavor stir-fries or soups, or to dip just-cooked ingredients from a hot pot. I have yet to meet a Taiwanese home cook who prepares this sauce rather than buying it in jars from a store. Yet the versions I've made are satisfying, and incorporate just a few rustic ingredients (without any additives like MSG). If you're up for the experiment and have a food processor, try this recipe for your own homemade sha-cha sauce instead of simply purchasing a jar. I've even made close-enough versions using salt cod instead of the dried brill fish that is a main ingredient in bottled Taiwanese versions. You can make your sauce as spicy as you like by increasing the amount of dried chilies in the recipe below, or slightly sweeter with the addition of more sugar. Keep it covered in an airtight container in the refrigerator for up to three months for the best flavor.

1 head garlic, coarsely chopped

4 medium shallots, coarsely chopped

6 to 8 small dried red chilies (preferably seven stars chilies, or substitute with chiles de arbol), seeds removed and roughly crumbled (about 1 tablespoon)

1 ounce dried stock fish (found in Asian groceries) or dried salt cod, torn into small pieces

1 ounce dried baby shrimp

½ cup vegetable or peanut oil

1 tablespoon sugar

½ teaspoon salt

1 teaspoon light soy sauce

Place the garlic and shallots in a food processor and pulse for a few seconds. Scrape down the sides with a rubber spatula and add the chilies, dried fish, and dried shrimp. Pulse, stopping to scrape down the sides with a spatula, for 2 to 3 minutes until the mixture becomes fine, evenly-sized crumbs.

Heat the oil in a small pot over medium heat. Add the chili mixture and cook, stirring frequently, for about 10 minutes. The mixture should resemble a golden, translucent sludge and the oil will have taken on a reddish-orange hue. Stir in the sugar and salt and continue cooking for another minute. Remove from the heat and stir in the soy sauce. Let cool completely before using.

Sweet-and-Sour Tomato–Based Sauce (Hai Shan Jiang)

海山醬

Makes about 1 cup

You won't go a few days in Taiwan without encountering this thick, red-tinged sauce. It's mild-tasting enough to liberally drench foods—like fried snacks—in a way that you couldn't with more potently flavored sauces like soy sauce or ketchup. This sauce relies heavily on ketchup, a condiment associated with Western food trends.

¼ cup ketchup

¼ cup rice vinegar

1 tablespoon sugar

1 teaspoon soy sauce

1 teaspoon cornstarch

½ cup cold water

Salt to taste

Add the ketchup, vinegar, sugar, and soy sauce to a small saucepan over medium-high heat and stir to combine thoroughly. Cook for a few seconds, stirring, until the sugar dissolves and the mixture is beginning to bubble. In a separate bowl, whisk together the cornstarch and water. Stir into the ketchup mixture and continue to cook, stirring, until thickened, about 1 minute. Add the salt to taste. Remove from the heat and let cool completely before serving.

Sweet-and-Sour Citrus and Soy–Based Sauce (Yang Sheng Zhan Jiang)

養生蘸醬

Makes about 1 cup

This sauce can be used interchangeably with Sweet-and-Sour Tomato–Based Sauce, such as for drizzling on tempura fishcakes. The use of fresh, tropical citrus juice is a given due to these fruits' availability on the island. The bright acidity of the resulting sauce makes it an excellent complement for savory, porky snacks like Meatball Mochi (see page 91).

¼ cup fresh orange juice

1 tablespoon fresh lime juice

1 tablespoon rice vinegar

1 tablespoon sugar, plus more to taste

2 teaspoons soy sauce

1 teaspoon cornstarch

½ cup cold water

Salt to taste

Add the orange juice, lime juice, vinegar, sugar, and soy sauce to a small saucepan over medium-high heat and stir to combine thoroughly. Cook, stirring, until the sugar dissolves and the mixture begins to boil. In a separate bowl, whisk together the cornstarch and water. Stir into the orange juice mixture and continue to cook, stirring, until thickened, about 1 minute. Add salt to taste. Taste for seasoning and add extra sugar or a pinch of salt as desired. Remove from the heat and let cool completely before serving.

Dumpling Dipping Sauce (Jiaozi Jiang)

餃子醬

Makes about ¼ cup

There is no such thing as the "best" or the "right way" to make a dipping sauce for dumplings, but this would be pretty on target. In reality, one can use soy sauce, vinegar (preferably aged or black vinegar, for its sweeter, mellower taste), thick soy sauce, their favorite chili sauce, or any combination of those to dip dumplings. But I prefer a fifty-fifty ratio of soy sauce and vinegar, which works well even if you only have sharper-tasting clear rice vinegar instead of aged. A dab of sesame oil adds savory depth and a flourish of ginger matchsticks on top can't hurt, either.

2 tablespoons light soy sauce

2 tablespoons rice vinegar

½ teaspoon sesame oil

1 teaspoon peeled and very thinly julienned fresh ginger (preferably young ginger, if you can find it)

Combine the soy sauce, vinegar, and oil in a sauce dish and scatter the ginger on top.

Pickled Mustard Greens (Zha Cai)

榨菜

Makes 2 quarts

There are numerous types of vegetables that are pickled until piquant and pucker-worthy in Taiwan. Chopped and tossed into noodle soup, congee, or scrambled with eggs, these salty bites are a convenient way to add flavor to rustic dishes. Chinese mustard greens, with their large, fibrous ribs and stems, are commonly pickled in a traditional lacto-fermented procedure (similar to making kimchi and sauerkraut). Most home cooks don't pickle their own mustard greens nowadays, as they're readily found premade in jars in Taiwan. But with about seven days' time and a lot of salt, a homemade version is simple.

1 head Chinese mustard greens, trimmed of any wilted leaves and tough stem at the base

¼ cup plus 2 tablespoons kosher salt or sea salt

4 cups water

In a large bowl or on a large plate, sprinkle the mustard greens evenly with 2 tablespoons of the salt. Let sit for 1 hour at room temperature. Rinse briefly under cold water and squeeze the mustard greens well to remove excess liquid.

In a large bowl, stir the remaining ¼ cup salt into the water until the salt is completely dissolved. Sterilize a 2-quart glass jar by completely submerging it in boiling water for 10 minutes. Remove carefully with tongs and drain. Stuff the mustard greens inside the jar (slicing them in half if necessary to fit). Pour the saltwater solution all the way to the top of the jar, making sure to submerge the greens. Cover with a lid. Keep away from light at room temperature until sufficiently tangy and briny tasting, 7 to 8 days (this may take as few as 5 days in the warm summer months, or up to 10 days in colder temperatures). You may open and close the jar to check on the progress in the meantime; the jar will open with an audible releasing of gases once it's fermented, and you may allow it to ferment longer for a stronger flavor. In general, I recommend 7 days of fermenting at room temperature. Afterward, store, airtight, in the refrigerator.

Mustard greens / Vinegar-Pickled Cabbage (page 61)

Pickled Mustard Greens Relish (Xue Cai)

雪菜

Makes ¼ cup

This simple relish incorporates the completed pickled mustard greens from page 57, seasoned with sesame oil and chili flakes for enhanced flavor.

¼ cup shredded Pickled Mustard Greens (see page 57)

2 teaspoons sesame oil

1 teaspoon light soy sauce

¼ teaspoon dried red chili flakes (optional)

Combine the mustard greens, sesame oil, soy sauce, and chili flakes, if using, in a small bowl and stir well. For the best flavor, store in an airtight container in the refrigerator for up to 3 months.

Vinegar-Pickled Cabbage (Suan Cai)

酸菜

Makes about 2 cups

Crunchy and tangy, these overnight pickles are often served as a cold appetizer or side dish. Their bright acidity makes for a great pairing with greasy or very strong-tasting foods, like fried wedges of Taiwanese stinky tofu.

1 pound green cabbage, coarsely shredded or torn into pieces no wider than 2 inches (yielding about 4 cups)

1 tablespoon kosher salt or sea salt

½ cup rice vinegar

¼ cup sugar

1 tablespoon peeled and julienned fresh ginger

1 to 2 small fresh red chilies, thinly sliced

In a large bowl, toss the cabbage with the salt. Let sit for 1 hour at room temperature. Rinse under cold water and squeeze well to remove excess liquid.

Heat the vinegar and sugar in a small saucepan over medium heat, stirring, just until the sugar is dissolved completely. Let cool completely to room temperature.

In a large bowl, toss the cabbage with the ginger, chilies, and vinegar solution. Mix well to distribute the liquid evenly and press into an airtight container. Refrigerate at least 10 hours before serving (preferably giving the cabbage a stir one or two times in between). For the best flavor, store, covered, in the refrigerator for up to 3 days.

Sweet Soy-Pickled Cucumbers (Yan Xiao Huang Gua)

醃小黃瓜

Makes about 2 cups

These pickles are stained deep brown from soy sauce and have a very sweet flavor, almost akin to gherkins. They're far more likely to be purchased rather than made at home, but they can be prepared using a simple method and classic Chinese ingredients. For best results, look for Asian cucumber varieties with crisp, nearly seedless interiors.

1 pound small pickling cucumbers, such as Persian cucumbers

2 teaspoons kosher salt or sea salt

½ cup rice vinegar

¼ cup dark soy sauce

¼ cup water

¼ cup sugar

1 star anise

Trim the ends from the cucumbers and chop into ½-inch pieces. In a large bowl, toss the cucumbers with the salt to coat thoroughly. Let sit for 30 minutes to 1 hour at room temperature. Rinse briefly under cold water. Drain and squeeze well to remove excess liquid.

Combine the vinegar, soy sauce, water, sugar, and star anise in a small saucepan over medium-high heat and bring just to a boil, stirring to thoroughly dissolve the sugar. Let cool completely to room temperature (or refrigerate, covered, overnight). Discard the star anise. Pour the mixture over the cucumbers in a large bowl or airtight container. Cover and refrigerate at least 24 hours before serving. Store, covered, in the refrigerator for up to 1 week.

Spicy Marinated Cucumbers (Suan La Xiao Huang Gua)

酸辣小黃瓜

Makes about 1 quart

There are endless ways to make a cold appetizer of marinated cucumbers in Taiwan, but any way you season them, they're a common sight at multicourse meals. I enjoy them with a fierce kick of garlic and chili sauce, and only a touch of sugar and acidity.

2 pounds cucumbers, peeled, seeded, and chopped

1 tablespoon kosher salt or sea salt

2 tablespoons rice vinegar

1 tablespoon sugar

4 garlic cloves, finely chopped

1 teaspoon sesame oil

1 tablespoon chili bean sauce

In a large bowl, sprinkle the cucumbers with the salt and toss to coat evenly. Let sit for 30 minutes to 1 hour at room temperature. Rinse briefly under cold water. Drain and squeeze well to remove excess liquid.

In a large bowl, stir together the vinegar, sugar, garlic, oil, and chili bean sauce, then fold in the cucumbers and toss to coat. Cover and refrigerate for at least 6 hours, or preferably 12 hours, before serving. For the best flavor, store, covered, in the refrigerator up to 2 days.

Crushed Peanut Powder (Hua Sheng Fen)

花生粉

Makes about ½ cup

Whether a topping for iced desserts, sautéed vegetables with garlic, bowls of noodles, or steamed buns, crushed peanuts are widely used in Taiwanese cuisine. This condiment is shared—along with fried shallots—with Taiwan's neighboring Southeast Asian cuisines. However, in Taiwan, the peanuts are usually found ground more finely, and are blended with sugar to create a powdery consistency. Be careful not to overmix the peanuts while using a blender or food processor, or else these loose crumbs will begin to bind into a pastelike consistency.

1 cup roasted unsalted shelled peanuts, skins removed

2 tablespoons sugar

Place the peanuts and sugar in a food processor or blender. Pulse until the mixture resembles coarse crumbs with some finer, powdery dust, about 1 minute, stopping to scrape down the sides intermittently. Store at room temperature, covered, for up to 1 week.

Appetizers
and
Street
Snacks

Flaky "clamshell" pastries

Taiwanese Pork Belly Buns (Gua Bao)

刈包

Makes 8

Often translated as "Taiwanese hamburger," this beloved street food has proven its international appeal. Popular variations are made by Taiwanese-American restaurants like BaoHaus and Fun Buns in the States. Most versions in Taiwan incorporate pork belly braised in a soy sauce-based broth like that of Pork Meat Sauce over Rice (page 180). I've suggested following the similar recipe for Red-Braised Pork Belly (page 183) for that juicy slab inside the bun. But no Gua Bao would be complete without its garnish of pickled mustard greens, chopped cilantro, and crushed peanuts. Bearing Hokkien and Hakka influences, it's a compact bite of wildly contrasting flavors and textures—and quintessentially Taiwanese. It sometimes goes by the nickname, "Tiger Bites Pig" in Taiwan for its mouth-like shape.

8 sandwich-style steamed buns (found in the refrigerated section of Asian groceries)

6 to 8 tablespoons chopped Pickled Mustard Greens (see page 57)

8 pieces Red-Braised Pork Belly (see page 183), sliced about ½ inch thick

¼ cup coarsely chopped fresh cilantro (stems included)

½ cup Crushed Peanut Powder (see page 63)

Steam the buns according to the package instructions. To assemble the buns, place a spoonful of mustard greens inside each bun, followed by a piece of pork belly. Top the pork belly with cilantro, followed by a pinch of the peanut powder. Serve immediately.

Peppery Pork Buns
(Hu Jiao Bing)
胡椒餅
Makes 8

This bun was popularized sometime after the mainlander influx of the late 1940s, with its invention claimed variously by a small handful of street vendors who have been making it for a couple generations. Patrons lining up at the stalls will be able to observe how the cooks add scallions to the meaty filling just before folding it all inside the dough; this makes the scallions extra fresh tasting and juicy. The buns' spiciness comes from a profusion of ground peppercorns. This bun is distinctive not only for its peppery bite, but also for the fact that it's baked. In Taiwan, you'll find them on street corners baked in deep portable ovens that resemble tandoori ovens. However, a home oven will turn out a golden-baked result as well.

For the crust

2 tablespoons warm water

1 teaspoon dry active yeast

½ teaspoon sugar

1 cup all-purpose flour, plus more for dusting

¼ teaspoon salt

1 tablespoon vegetable or peanut oil

½ cup water

For the filling

½ pound ground pork

½ teaspoon ground white pepper

½ teaspoon ground black pepper

½ teaspoon ground Sichuan peppercorns or substitute with more black pepper

1 teaspoon sesame oil

1 teaspoon light soy sauce

¼ teaspoon salt

To continue

3 to 4 whole scallions, trimmed and finely chopped

½ cup sesame seeds

Make the crust

In a small bowl, combine the 2 tablespoons warm water with the yeast and sugar and stir to dissolve. Let stand at room temperature until frothy, 5 minutes.

Sift the flour and salt into a large bowl. Stir in the yeast mixture, oil and enough of the ½ cup water that the dough just comes together when stirred. Turn onto a floured surface and knead the dough until smooth to the touch, 6 to 8 minutes. Place the dough in a bowl and cover with a kitchen towel. Let rest in a warm area until the dough has risen to about twice its bulk, 45 minutes to 1 hour.

Make the filling

Meanwhile, in a large bowl, combine the pork, white pepper, black pepper, Sichuan peppercorns, oil, soy sauce, and salt. Mix to combine thoroughly by hand (the mixture can be covered and refrigerated overnight).

Preheat the oven to 350°F. Transfer the dough onto a lightly floured surface. With your hands, roll the dough into a snake and then cut the dough into 8 evenly sized pieces. Roll out each piece into a flat round about four inches in diameter.

To continue

Scoop about a tablespoon of the scallions into the center of each round, followed by another tablespoon of the seasoned pork mixture. Carefully bring the edges of the dough to the center of the bun to seal it shut over the filling. Make sure there are no gaps or holes. Place the buns sealed-side down on a baking sheet.

Once all the buns have been formed, scatter the sesame seeds on a flat plate. Place another plate next to it and fill with a very thin pool of water. Dip the tops of each bun into the water and then the sesame seeds, and return to the baking sheet, spacing each bun 2 inches apart. Bake until the tops are lightly golden brown, about 30 minutes. Let cool, preferably on a wire rack, for a few minutes before serving.

Pan-Fried Leek Buns with Dried Shrimp (Jiu Cai Shui Jian Bao)

韭菜水煎包

Makes 8

Pan-fried buns are a common snack in Taiwan. Similar to pan-fried dumplings, they're crisped until golden on the bottom, yet steamed through so that the filling cooks along with the noodlelike dough. They're stuffed with numerous fillings, from vegetable-based ones like this classic green leek version accented with a hint of chopped dried baby shrimp, to juicy pork-based versions. Typically, this version would be made with deep-green, flat-shaped Chinese chives, also called Chinese leeks, which can be found in Asian markets. However, the delicate, springlike flavor of larger common leeks found in the States is lovely, too, even if the leeks aren't as vibrant in color. I've also incorporated clear mung bean noodles in the filling, which absorbs the rest of the flavors and makes the filling slightly easier to form into neat packages. (Recipe featured on cover.)

For the crust

1 cup all-purpose flour, plus more for dusting

¼ teaspoon salt

1 tablespoon vegetable or peanut oil

⅓ cup water

For the filling

1 tablespoon dried baby shrimp

4 to 6 large leeks, white and light green parts only, or 1 large bunch whole Chinese chives or leeks

2 tablespoons vegetable or peanut oil

½ teaspoon salt, plus more to taste

¼ lb dried mung bean starch noodles (bean thread noodles)

1 teaspoon sesame oil

¼ teaspoon ground white pepper, plus more to taste

To continue

2 tablespoons vegetable or peanut oil, for pan-frying

½ cup water

Dumpling Dipping Sauce (see page 56)

For the crust

Combine the flour and salt in a large bowl. Stir in the oil and enough of the water so that the dough just comes together in a ball. Turn the dough onto a floured surface and knead until the surface is smooth, 6 to 8 minutes. Cover with plastic and set aside to rest for 20 to 30 minutes.

For the filling

In a small bowl, soak the dried shrimp in about ¼ cup water for at least 5 minutes, until slightly softened. Drain and chop finely. Finely chop the leeks.

Heat the vegetable oil in a large skillet or wok over medium-high heat. Once hot, add the soaked shrimp and cook, stirring, until fragrant, about 30 seconds. Add the leeks along with the salt and cook, stirring occasionally, until softened and the juices have mostly evaporated, 8 to 10 minutes. You should have about 1 cup of the leek mixture.

Cook the noodles according to the package instructions. Drain well. Once cool enough to handle, transfer to a cutting board and coarsely chop. You should have about 1 cup chopped noodles.

In a bowl, combine the cooked leek mixture and the noodles. Stir in the sesame oil and white pepper and taste for seasoning, adding extra salt and white pepper as desired.

To form the buns, divide the dough into eight equal-sized pieces. Roll out each one on a slightly floured surface to a round about 4 inches in diameter. Place about 1 tablespoon filling in the center of each round. Carefully bring the edges of the dough to the center of the bun to seal it shut over the filling. Make sure there are no gaps or holes. Place the buns sealed-side down on a lightly floured surface as each one is finished.

To continue

Heat the oil in a large skillet with a lid over medium-high heat. Once hot, arrange as many buns as will fit in a single layer in the pan so that the bottoms retain full contact with the pan (you may need to work in batches). Cook until the bottoms are just golden brown, 2 to 3 minutes. Add the water and immediately cover the pan. Steam until the dough on the tops of the buns has turned translucent rather than opaque white, about 8 minutes. If there is still liquid remaining in the pan, uncover and continue to cook until it evaporates. Serve immediately, on their own or with the dipping sauce.

Flaky Daikon Radish Pastries (Luo Bo Si Bing)

蘿蔔絲餅

Makes 8

This savory bun, like so many others, may be filled with various meat- or vegetable-based fillings, but it is unique for its rich, buttery crust. This filling of shredded daikon is cooked a long time to ensure that it becomes very dry and concentrated in flavor. If it is too wet, the mixture will burst through the delicate crust as it bakes, although small gushes that occur while baking in the oven are no problem. These buns are sometimes called "clamshell buns" because of their diminutive, bloated shapes.

For the crust

1 stick (½ cup) cold unsalted butter

1¼ cups all-purpose flour, plus more for dusting

½ teaspoon baking powder

¼ teaspoon salt

1 tablespoon cold water

For the filling

2 tablespoons vegetable or peanut oil

2 cups packed peeled and finely shredded daikon radish

Salt and ground white pepper to taste

For the crust

Cut the butter into small cubes. In a large bowl or in the bowl of a food processor, combine the flour, baking powder, and salt and then cut in the butter using a pastry cutter or by pulsing the food processor several times. Continue until the mixture resembles coarse crumbs no larger than peas. Sprinkle in just enough of the water until the mixture comes together in a ball. Cover with plastic wrap and refrigerate for at least 15 minutes.

For the filling

Meanwhile, heat the oil in a large skillet or wok over high heat. Add the daikon and a pinch of salt. Cook, stirring occasionally, until the daikon has released and cooked off its liquid, 20 to 30 minutes. Taste and add extra salt and white pepper as desired. Let cool completely. If the mixture still appears somewhat wet after cooling, squeeze out any excess liquid.

Preheat the oven to 375°F. Cut the chilled dough into 8 evenly sized pieces. To form the pastries, press out a piece of dough on a lightly floured surface into a round about 3 inches in diameter. Fill with a spoonful of the radish mixture, not quite one tablespoon. Carefully bring the edges of the dough to the center of the bun to seal it shut over the filling. Place the buns sealed-side down on a baking sheet, spacing them about 2 inches apart. Bake until the tops are lightly golden brown, 20 to 25 minutes. Let cool, preferably on a wire rack, for a few moments before serving hot and fresh from the oven.

Pan-Fried Pork and Napa Cabbage Pot Stickers (Guotie)

鍋貼

Makes about 36

Lucky you who eats many of these crispy, golden dumplings. The shape of a Taiwanese pot sticker is similar to the ancient golden ingot, so they are associated with good fortune and prosperity. In street-made versions of guotie in Taiwan, the pan-fried dumplings are often very long, thin, and opened at the edges rather than strictly sealed. I've asked many why this was so, and have gotten practical answers ranging from "they're quicker and easier to fold" to "the oil would splatter up into your face while cooking otherwise." These are valid points; however, when making pan-fried dumplings at home, one need not worry about packing many of them into one pan or ensuring a quicker cooking time, as vendors would. Therefore, I encourage making fully closed, pinch-sealed pot stickers from freshly kneaded dough if you're going through the effort of making dumplings.

For the filling

1 pound ground pork

4 whole scallions, trimmed and finely chopped

1 cup packed finely shredded napa cabbage

1 tablespoon peeled and grated fresh ginger

2 teaspoons light soy sauce

1 teaspoon cornstarch

¼ teaspoon salt

¼ teaspoon ground white pepper

For the wrappers

2 cups all-purpose flour, plus more for dusting

1 cup cold water

To continue

2 tablespoons vegetable or peanut oil, for pan-frying

½ cup water

Dumpling Dipping Sauce (see page 56)

Continued on next page

1. *Kneaded dough is brushed with flour*

2. *Then pressed and rolled out*

3. *Filling is spread along center*

4. *A pinch is made on opposite ends*

5. *Another pich is made along the edge to the right of center*

6. *And another to the right of that*

7. *Continue until the right-hand side of the dumpling is sealed with pinches*

8. *Starting from the center, repeat process along the left side*

9. *Pinch the edges until you reach the end*

10. *Ensure that each pinch is fully sealed*

11. *Repeat with remaining dough and filling*

For the filling

In a large bowl, combine the pork, scallions, cabbage, ginger, soy sauce, cornstarch, salt, and white pepper and mix with your hands. You can do this up to a day ahead and store, covered, in the refrigerator.

For the wrappers

To make the dough, place the flour in a large bowl. Stir in enough of the water so that the dough just comes together. Turn onto a floured surface and knead the dough until very smooth on the surface, 6 to 8 minutes. Cover with plastic wrap and let rest for 20 minutes.

To assemble the dumplings, take a knob of dough, about 1 tablespoon, and press it onto a floured surface. Roll it out from the center to the edges into a relatively round disc about 4 inches in diameter. Scoop a tablespoon of the filling onto the center of the round. Bring two opposite edges of the wrapper together over the center of the filling and pinch. Holding it from the center, fold and pinch the dough as shown until the edge is fully sealed. Starting about half an inch right of the center, bring a piece of the edge toward the center and pinch it closed. Bring another piece, about half an inch to the right of the last pinch, toward the center and pinch it closed. Repeat with one or two more pinches along the right edge of the dumpling until the side is fully sealed at the top. Repeat process with the left side of the dumpling, until the top edge is fully sealed. Place the dumpling on a floured surface, with the pinched seam on top. Repeat with the remaining dough and filling.

To continue

Heat the oil in a large skillet with a lid over medium-high heat. Arrange the dumplings in a spiral shape from the outer edge of the pan toward the center (to fit the most dumplings in one batch). Ensure that the undersides of all the dumplings have full contact with the pan. Cook just until the bottoms of the dumplings are lightly golden brown, about 2 minutes. Add the water and immediately cover the pan. Steam until the wrappers have all turned translucent instead of opaque white, 8 to 10 minutes. If there is still liquid remaining on the bottom of the pan, uncover and continue to cook just until it evaporates. Turn onto a platter and serve with the dipping sauce.

Beaten eggs are poured over the oysters

Form into a pancake-sized shape

Starch slurry is poured over

The omelet is flipped to lightly brown the opposite side

Drizzle with sauce and serve

Oyster Omelet
(E Zai Jian / O Ah Jian)

蚵仔煎

Makes 2

This dish is rooted in Fujian cuisine, but nowhere is it enjoyed with as great enthusiasm as in Taiwan. Found at night markets as well as made in average homes, it's a rustic snack that features one of Taiwan's most plentiful (and favorite) seafood—oysters. Tasting the dish from a vendor in a coastal region where oysters are caught nearby, however, can be a night-and-day difference from tasting it from a vendor far from the coast. That's because oysters are typically preshucked when purchased from seafood markets, and can be somewhat bland-tasting compared to freshly shucked ones. To get the full experience of the briny bivalves, I'd recommend learning to shuck oysters and buying them whole in the shell for this recipe. Only a few oysters are needed for an oyster omelet, and their flavor becomes absorbed in the egg mixture and jellylike starch slurry. This delicacy has much to do with enjoying the soft, gelatinous textures of the oysters and clear, starchy gel.

4 large eggs

Pinch each of salt and ground white pepper

1 to 2 tablespoons vegetable or peanut oil

8 oysters, preshucked or shucked at home

1 tablespoon sweet potato starch

½ cup cold water

1 small head baby bok choy or
other mild-tasting leafy green, shredded

1 whole scallion, trimmed and finely chopped

Sweet-and-Sour Tomato–Based Sauce (see page 54)

In a small bowl, beat the eggs with the salt and white pepper. Heat 1 tablespoon of the oil in a skillet over high heat. Once the oil is very hot and starting to pop a little, add 4 of the oysters to the pan. Let cook until they appear more firm, about 1 minute.

Stir the sweet potato starch into the cold water in a small bowl. Pour half the mixture into the pan over the oysters. Let bubble for a couple seconds and then pour half the beaten egg mixture into the pan over the oyster mixture. Let bubble for a few seconds while scraping the running edges toward the center to form a rounder, neater shape about 5 to 6 inches in diameter. Place half the bok choy and scallion on top of the omelet. Peek at the underside of the omelet by lifting with a spatula and loosen the edges all around. If the underside is lightly browned and the edges are all loose, carefully flip the entire omelet over (use two spatulas if needed). Cook on the opposite side to lightly brown, about 1 more minute. Invert onto a plate to serve with the vegetable side facing up. Drizzle the top liberally with the sauce and serve immediately. Repeat the process with the remaining ingredients.

Coffin Cake
(Guan Cai Ban)
棺材板

Makes 4

This unusual snack is clearly inspired by foreign culinary influences. Its thick, creamy filling resembles a chicken corn chowder, and it's served in a fat slice of fried Japanese white bread. Yet its playful construction is strictly Taiwanese: this snack is named "coffin bread" or "coffin cake" because the bread is cut to flap over like the lid of a coffin. The inventor of coffin cake showed a sense of humor when creating it, poking fun at ancestor worship and mortality.

For the filling

1 cup frozen sweet corn kernels, thawed

½ cup frozen green peas, thawed

½ cup diced carrots

2 to 3 small squid, cleaned and sliced into rings and tentacles coarsely chopped

2 cups whole milk

2 tablespoons unsalted butter

2 tablespoons all-purpose flour

1 cup gently shredded precooked chicken meat (trimmed of any skin and bone)

1 whole scallion, trimmed and finely chopped

½ teaspoon salt

¼ teaspoon ground white pepper

To continue

2 to 3 cups vegetable or peanut oil, for deep-frying

4 slices Japanese white bread or brioche, cut about 1½ inches thick

For the filling

Bring a small pot of lightly salted water to a boil. Blanch the corn, peas, and carrots for 3 to 4 minutes and drain thoroughly. Next, blanch the squid until opaque, about 1 minute, and drain thoroughly.

In a small pot, heat the milk over medium-low until warm, but not boiling. In a separate saucepan, melt the butter over medium-high heat. Stir in the flour and cook, stirring frequently, until frothy and bubbling, about 1 minute.

Slowly pour the milk into the butter and flour mixture while whisking rapidly. Continue whisking until the mixture begins to bubble and thicken and to eliminate lumps. Once thick and bubbling, stir in the cooked vegetables, chicken, scallion, salt and pepper. Warm the mixture through and taste for seasoning, adding salt and pepper as desired. Stir in the blanched squid last to ensure that it doesn't overcook. Remove from the heat.

To continue

Add enough oil to a deep saucepan or wok so that it's deep enough to submerge at least half the thickness of the bread. Heat over medium-high heat until a candy thermometer inserted into the oil (but not touching the pan) reads between 325° to 350°F. Drop in the bread one slice at a time. Fry until crisp and golden on one side, then flip over with tongs to brown the opposite side. Let cool on paper towels. Repeat with the remaining slices.

Create the "lids" on the tops of the bread slices: using a paring knife, gently score the top of each slice about a quarter-inch from the edge on three sides. Using a cleaver or chef's knife, cut out the lid from the three scored edges, slicing approximately halfway through the thickness of the bread and leaving the fourth edge intact (like a hinge). You should have a lid that flaps open like a book and a rim around the remaining three sides of the slice. Using a spatula, gently flip over the lid to expose the bread inside. Repeat with the remaining slices. Ladle a scoop of the filling inside each piece of bread and serve immediately.

Taiwan's Night Markets

For Taiwanese city dwellers, eating and shopping are everyday social activities. Nowhere is this more vivid than at night markets—swarming, claustrophobic street fairs that occur every evening until past midnight. These markets consume entire streets, with people flocking every storefront like an open-air sidewalk sale. Vendors sell everything from ready-to-eat foods to clothing, electronics, household goods, and even pets. To each neighborhood, its own type of night market, but in cities with universities, you can be sure there are trendy shops and eateries catering to the youthful clientele—some just dawdling and window-shopping, or simply grabbing snacks on the go.

Patrons enjoying a street vendor's stand

It might seem like night markets epitomize the capitalist culture that has overwhelmed upwardly mobile Taiwanese youngsters. But in fact, night markets spun off of a much simpler, age-old tradition. It's no coincidence that some of the earliest such markets originated near the cities' temples. Tainan, which boasts a robust night market scene of several blocks surrounding its oldest temple, stands testament to this institution. Street food vendors began setting up camp around it to serve worshippers leaving the temple. To attract more customers and set themselves apart from their competitors, these food vendors would try to outdo one another by serving up the most original and tasty offerings.

Taiwan is a deeply religious society as a whole, and it should be noted that visiting temples frequently is not a thing of the past. Unhindered by the Communist Cultural Revolution that took place on mainland China, ancient religions and the customs that are practiced within them have continued to flourish on the island. In general, these consist of Buddhism and Taoism, with folk religious beliefs sprinkled in. Many Taiwanese worship folk deities that are Taoist in origin for various purposes throughout the year—such as having children or to promote good crops for the season. Major religious holidays usually call for abundant family meals, with certain foods enjoyed to observe each one.

But as an everyday ritual, tasting from cart after cart outside a temple became a leisure activity. It has greatly contributed to the dramatic array of delights seen in the Taiwanese culinary landscape. It continues to grow today—the last time I visited Taiwan, I tried a novel creation of a grilled chicken wing that was stuffed underneath the skin with sticky rice. Served with a split top to expose the filling, it was topped with a colorful garnish of fresh scallions and pickled sliced chilies. Intrepid market vendors like these are responsible for many of the popular favorites among Taiwanese signature foods—like the cilantro and crushed peanut–topped pork belly buns, fried chicken bites, and coffin cakes.

Taiwanese night market food is constantly evolving, and expanding the realm of its cuisine as a whole. Not all the food is newfangled, and popular standbys have remained. For instance, one can get a bowl of rou geng (page 130) with any number of additions, such as meatballs and fish cakes, ladled and scooped to order. This service style is also fitting for the tradition of lu wei–braised snack foods. Similar to hot pot, lu wei consists of multiple snacks—such as fish cakes, meatballs, fried tofu cubes, offal, taro root and other vegetables—that are dipped in a boiling soy sauce and five-spice-flavored broth. Once taken out of the broth, the bite-sized morsels have absorbed the broth's flavor and can be eaten with a toothpick for easy snacking (for a more robust meal, noodles may also be dipped into the broth and added to the fixin's). The method is simple, but it requires a deeply flavorful broth, and that broth only becomes richer the more things are dipped into it.

Despite all the newfangled food crazes found at night markets, these and many other traditional Taiwanese-style foods remain just as popular with young eaters as older patrons, making the night market scene a uniquely and distinctively Taiwanese institution.

A bowl of assorted lu wei–stewed food

Tea Eggs
(Cha Ye Dan)
茶葉蛋

Makes 1 dozen

Marbled, soy sauce and tea–stained eggs are literally everywhere in Taiwan—there's a convenience store serving them up from slow-cookers on every city corner. However, tea eggs predate convenience stores as a popular snack. They're similar to stewed eggs, which are simply hard-boiled eggs dropped into a soy sauce and five-spice–accented broth to absorb its flavor over several hours. Other ingredients may be dropped into this broth as well, like tofu, fish cakes, or duck feet, to acquire a mahogany sheen and deep flavor (lu wei cooking). Tea eggs are hard-boiled and then not peeled but cracked all over, so that color seeps through their porous shells in crackled patterns. To help this dyeing process, black tea leaves are added to the broth, which lends an appealing flavor.

1 dozen large eggs

8 cups water

½ cup dark soy sauce

¼ cup packed loose black tea leaves

2 teaspoons five-spice powder

1 star anise

Place the eggs carefully in a large pot and fill with water just to cover. Bring to a boil over high heat and allow to boil for 5 minutes. Drain the water, and when just cool enough to handle, crack the eggs all around with the underside of a spoon.

Place the eggs in the drained pot and add the 8 cups water, soy sauce, tea leaves, five-spice powder, and star anise. Bring to a boil, then reduce the heat to a low simmer. Simmer, covered, for at least 2 hours to acquire a marbled staining underneath the shells. The coloring becomes deeper the longer it is cooked. Store the eggs in the broth to refrigerate in between heating up and serving. Keep refrigerated no longer than 5 days.

Fried Chicken Bites (Yan Su Ji)

鹽酥雞

Makes about 4 servings

Crispy, boneless pieces of fried chicken are a likely street food obsession. Quick and easy to serve up by a single cart, these hot and delicious bites are what we might call "popcorn chicken." Taiwanese fried chicken bites are distinct in a few ways, however: the meat is marinated with five-spice powder and the pieces sprinkled generously with salt and white pepper once out of the oil. They're often served along with fried leaves of basil as an attractive garnish. So crisp and flavorful on their own, they're not often accompanied with a dipping sauce.

For the chicken

1 pound boneless, skinless chicken breasts, cut into 1-inch pieces

1 teaspoon light soy sauce

¼ teaspoon five-spice powder

¼ teaspoon salt

¼ teaspoon ground white pepper

½ teaspoon cornstarch

3 to 4 cups vegetable or peanut oil, or more as needed, for frying

For the breading

2 large eggs, lightly beaten

1 cup water

½ cup sweet potato starch

1 bunch fresh Thai basil leaves

Salt and ground white pepper to taste

For the chicken

In a large bowl, marinate the chicken pieces with the soy sauce, five-spice powder, salt, white pepper, and cornstarch. You can do this up to a day ahead and store, covered, in the refrigerator.

Add the oil to a saucepan or wok so that it is deep enough to completely submerge the pieces of chicken (add more oil if necessary). Heat over medium-high heat until a candy thermometer inserted into the oil (but not touching the pan) reads between 350° and 375°F. When cooking, adjust the heat if necessary to retain this temperature.

For the breading

Combine the eggs with the water in a bowl. Place the sweet potato starch in another bowl next to it. Dip each piece of chicken into the egg wash first, followed by the starch. Shake off any excess. Drop the pieces into the oil one small batch (about 8 pieces) at a time and let fry, turning them occasionally with tongs, until crispy and golden all around, 2 to 3 minutes. Remove the chicken with a slotted spoon and transfer immediately to paper towels. Once all the chicken has been fried, carefully drop in the bunch of basil and fry for a few seconds just until crisp and translucent. Remove and transfer immediately to paper towels. Sprinkle the chicken pieces generously with salt and white pepper to taste and serve immediately with the fried basil leaves.

Taiwanese Grilled Corn (Kao Yu Mi)

烤玉米

Makes 4

Corn on the cob isn't enjoyed too often in Taiwan, but a certain grilled version is found as a street food snack. In Keelung's temple food market strip, it's an exciting specialty. The corn is stripped of its husks and brushed generously with a sweet soy and sha-cha sauce mixture. It's grilled on a stick until the marinade is nearly burned all over, creating a hard shellac that's somewhat chewy, yet delicious. The best thing about making this dish outside of Taiwan is that the corn in Taiwan is starchy and not very flavorful; sweet corn found in the late summer in the States makes this treat even tastier.

2 teaspoons Sha-Cha Sauce (see page 53)

¼ cup light soy sauce

1 tablespoon vegetable or peanut oil

1 teaspoon sugar

4 ears sweet corn, shucked

In a small bowl, combine the sha-cha sauce, soy sauce, oil, and sugar and stir thoroughly. Insert a skewer into the end of each corn cob. Grill the corn, turning it occasionally, until nearly fully cooked, about 5 minutes. Brush the corn liberally with the sauce, and continue to grill, turning to blister and slightly blacken all the sides and brushing on even more sauce, for another 2 to 3 minutes. Serve on the stick.

Meatball Mochi (Ba-Wan / Rou Yuan)

Makes 4 to 6

This traditional southern Taiwanese snack incorporates many Taiwanese penchants: a chewy, jellylike starch; a thick, sweetened sauce; and a savory, pork-studded filling. This dish is translated as "meatball" in Taiwan, but it's actually a ball of clear, stretchy starch stuffed with meat. So I took the liberty of naming it "meatball mochi"—due to its similarities with the soft, chewy stuffed dessert.

For the filling

½ pound pork shoulder, finely chopped

½ cup finely chopped fresh bamboo shoots (see Note, page 159), or canned, rinsed well

1 teaspoon light soy sauce

½ teaspoon cornstarch

¼ teaspoon salt

¼ teaspoon ground white pepper

For the wrapper

½ cup rice flour

1 cup cold water

2 cups boiling water

½ cup sweet potato starch

1 cup corn starch

To continue

Vegetable or peanut oil, for greasing bowls

Sweet-and-Sour Tomato–Based Sauce (see page 54) or Sweet-and-Sour Citrus and Soy–Based Sauce (see page 55)

½ bunch coarsely chopped fresh cilantro (stems included)

For the filling

In a large bowl, combine the pork, bamboo shoots, soy sauce, cornstarch, salt, and white pepper. You can do this up to a day ahead and store, covered, in the refrigerator.

For the wrapper

In a large bowl, combine the rice flour and ¼ cup of the cold water and mix until smooth. Whisk in the boiling water and stir well to eliminate any lumps and create a milky, translucent, thick liquid. Combine the sweet potato starch, cornstarch, and the remaining ¾ cup cold water in a separate bowl. Pour this mixture into the warm rice flour mixture and stir thoroughly until the mixture is thick and there are no lumps (if there are many visible lumps, strain the mixture through a colander).

To continue

Prepare a large steamer with boiling water underneath. Grease the insides of four small, round ramekins (or rice bowls or round sauce dishes) with oil. Scoop about 1 tablespoon of the mochi mixture and spread it on the bottom of the bowl. Place a small scoop of the filling on top of the mixture, followed by another scoop of the mochi mixture. Spread it over to cover the meat mixture completely. Place the bowls in the steamer and steam until the starch is clear and set, about 15 minutes. Remove the bowls carefully. Ladle a scoop of your preferred sauce over each ball and top with the cilantro to serve.

Sticky rice steamed inside bamboo

Molded Sticky Rice (Tong Zai Mi Gao)

筒仔米糕

Makes 4 to 6 servings

Seasoned sticky rice tossed with bits of meat and slivered vegetables is an appealing comfort food throughout Taiwan as well as China. It can be stuffed inside lotus leaves and steamed, as a famous snack served on the holiday known as Tomb-Sweeping Day or Qing Ming, or it can be stuffed inside bamboo logs and steamed, as aboriginal Taiwanese often do. Here, it's simply molded in a round bowl and inverted onto a plate. The Taiwanese love to drizzle it with sauce and sprinkle it with fresh cilantro afterward. Look for rice labeled "sweet rice," which is stickier than common short-grain rice. As a substitute, I've used sushi rice with good results for this dish, too.

½ pound pork shoulder, sliced into long slivers

1 teaspoon light soy sauce

½ teaspoon cornstarch

¼ teaspoon salt, plus more to taste

¼ teaspoon ground white pepper, plus more to taste

1 cup sweet rice

¼ cup vegetable or peanut oil

4 to 5 dried shiitake mushrooms, soaked in cold water until fully reconstituted (about 30 minutes), de-stemmed and sliced

½ cup julienned carrots

½ cup julienned fresh bamboo shoots (see Note, page 159) or canned, rinsed well

2 tablespoons Fried Shallots (see page 52)

For serving

Vegetable or peanut oil, for greasing bowls

Sweet-and-Sour Tomato–Based Sauce (see page 54) or Sweet and Sour Citrus and Soy–Based Sauce (see page 55)

½ bunch coarsely chopped fresh cilantro (stems included)

In a large bowl, combine the pork with the soy sauce, cornstarch, salt, and white pepper and mix thoroughly. You can do this up to a day ahead and store, covered, in the refrigerator.

Steam the rice according to the package instructions.

Heat 2 tablespoons of the oil in a large skillet or wok over medium-high heat. Add the marinated pork and cook, stirring frequently, until just opaque and cooked through, 1 to 2 minutes. Transfer to a bowl and set aside. Toss the mushrooms, carrots, and bamboo shoots into the same wok and cook, stirring, until the carrots are just softened, 1 to 2 minutes. Return the pork to the wok and add the remaining 2 tablespoons oil. Heat just until the oil begins to bubble.

Turn off the heat and stir in all the rice and the fried shallots. Mix thoroughly with a spatula and season generously with salt and white pepper. Taste for seasoning, adding salt and white pepper as desired.

For serving

Lightly grease 4 to 6 rice bowls (or small round ramekins) with oil. Scoop the rice mixture into the bowls, packing and pressing down as much as will fit. Invert each bowl onto a plate. Top with your preferred sauce and the cilantro to serve.

Taiwanese Burrito (Run Bing)

潤餅

Makes 4

It's no Tex-Mex, but this handheld snack does resemble a burrito in its construction. Commonly found at street markets, but often made at the family table as well, these wraps are stuffed with plenty of shredded vegetables and minimal amounts of meat or scrambled egg. They're great for using up leftover scraps, or for eating on the go. The silky, stretchy wrappers are easy to roll up lots of fillings. Many street vendors in Taiwan will make theirs from scratch, but in homes, a package of fresh spring roll wrappers is usually the preferred option, since making them would require a large, flat griddle. Look for round, thin, white spring roll wrappers in the refrigerated section of an Asian market.

2 tablespoons vegetable or peanut oil

2 large eggs

Salt and ground white pepper to taste

4 cups shredded napa cabbage

2 cups julienned carrots

2 cups fresh bean sprouts

4 fresh (8-inch) round spring roll wrappers

1 to 2 cups shredded leftover roast pork or chicken

1 bunch fresh cilantro, coarsely chopped

2 tablespoons Crushed Peanut Powder (see page 63)

Heat 1 tablespoon of the oil in a large skillet or wok over high heat. In a bowl, beat the eggs and season them with a pinch each of salt and white pepper. Once the oil is hot, pour the eggs in the pan and stir immediately with a spatula. Cook, stirring to scramble and break up the eggs into small chunks, about 1 minute. Transfer the eggs to a bowl and set aside.

Rinse the pan and wipe dry. Heat the remaining tablespoon of oil over high heat and once hot, add the cabbage. Season with a pinch each of salt and pepper and cook, stirring frequently, until the cabbage has mostly wilted, about 2 minutes. Add the carrots and bean sprouts and cook, stirring, until the bean sprouts are translucent, about 2 minutes more. Add extra salt and white pepper to taste. Transfer the vegetables to a bowl and set aside.

To assemble each roll, spread a spring roll wrapper on a flat surface. Arrange one-quarter of the vegetable mixture in a horizontal line across the center of the roll, stopping at least 1 inch from the edges. Distribute one-quarter of the pork or chicken and then one-quarter of the scrambled eggs on top of the vegetables. Scatter one-quarter of the chopped cilantro and one-quarter of the peanut powder on top of the filling. Fold the two short edges of the wrapper over the filling mixture. Fold the bottom edge over all the filling, then press firmly and roll the filling bundle until it is fully enclosed in the wrapper. Repeat with the remaining wrappers and filling.

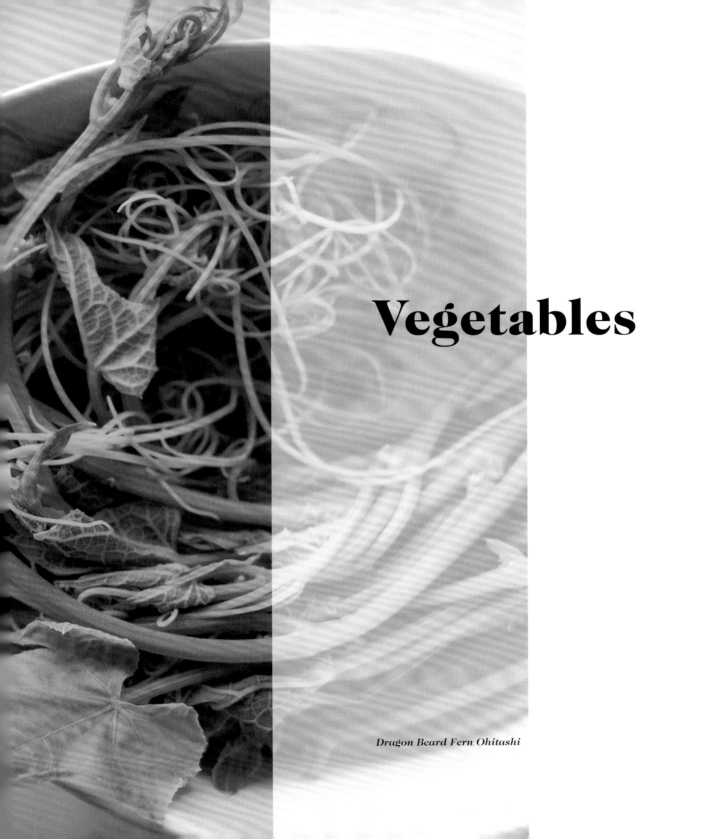

Vegetables

Dragon Beard Fern Ohitashi

Dried Radish Omelet (Cai Fu Dan)

菜脯蛋

Makes about 4 servings

This home-style dish is rustic and very minimal, but it's such a beloved comfort food that you'll find it on many restaurant menus in Taiwan. It incorporates dried, salt-cured daikon radish strips, which are chopped finely and fried in oil before being covered with beaten eggs. The chewy, salty, and very tasty little morsels are studded throughout the omelet. The best versions are made very quickly and with skill to create a very deep, fluffy, round cake—almost like a frittata. It's fun and easy to master at home.

¼ cup finely chopped dried daikon radish (found in Asian groceries)

6 large eggs

¼ teaspoon salt

¼ teaspoon ground white pepper

2 tablespoons water

2 tablespoons vegetable or peanut oil

Rinse the chopped dried radish in cold water. Squeeze to drain and pat dry with paper towels. (For less salty pieces, the chopped dried radish can also be soaked in water for 5 to 10 minutes before draining and drying.)

In a bowl, whisk the eggs with the salt, white pepper, and water.

Heat the oil in a large skillet or wok over medium-high, until the oil is very hot and begins to pop a little. Stir in the dried radish and cook, stirring, for about 30 seconds. Pour in the beaten eggs. Scrape the edges that are beginning to cook toward the center of the pan to create ruffles of gently cooked eggs in a tall, round heap. Loosen the edges of the omelet with a spatula. Once the eggs are almost thoroughly set on top and the underside of the omelet appears to be golden brown, carefully flip the entire omelet over. Cook on the opposite side until lightly browned, about 1 more minute. Transfer to a serving dish and serve immediately.

Tomato Salad with Ginger-Soy Dip (Liang Ban Fan Qie)

涼拌番茄

Makes about 2 servings

Fresh tomatoes are available in multiple heirloom colors and sizes in Taiwan. Because of their natural sweetness, they're often found cut up in fruit salads or served with ice cream or shaved ice desserts. Hey, tomatoes are technically a fruit. This fresh, minimal salad is the perfect way to open the palate for a multicourse meal. It's served with a somewhat Japanese-inspired sauce of thick soy sauce with a lot of grated fresh ginger swimming on top. If you can't find thick soy sauce (see page 47), opt for oyster sauce or just soy sauce instead.

1 tablespoon thick soy sauce

1 teaspoon peeled and grated fresh ginger

3 ripe yet firm tomatoes, cut into wedges

Place the soy sauce in a sauce dish and top with the ginger. Serve alongside the tomato wedges for dipping.

Steamed Eggplant with Garlic and Chilies (Suan Rong Qie Zi)

蒜茸茄子

Makes about 2 servings

Long, tender chunks of Asian eggplant are absolutely delightful when steamed through. Their flesh cooks to a custardlike softness, without absorbing too much oil like they do when cooked in a pan. This is a typical Taiwanese preparation that's not for those averse to strong flavor: lots of fresh garlic and often chopped fresh red chilies and scallions are sprinkled liberally on the steamed eggplant as an attractive and very tasty garnish.

2 long slender Asian eggplants, about 1 pound

¼ teaspoon salt

4 garlic cloves, minced

1 scallion, chopped

4 to 5 small fresh red chilies, seeded and chopped (optional)

2 tablespoons light soy sauce

Prepare a large bamboo steamer with boiling water underneath.

Trim the ends from the eggplant and cut into halves lengthwise. Sprinkle with the salt and arrange in the steamer. Cover the steamer and let cook until the eggplants feel soft to the touch all around, 8 to 10 minutes. Arrange the eggplant skin-side down on a serving dish. Sprinkle the garlic, scallions, and optional chilies over each piece followed by a drizzle of the soy sauce and serve immediately.

Sautéed King Oyster Mushrooms with Ginger (Qing Chao Xing Bao Gu)

清炒杏鮑菇

Makes about 4 servings

Juicy, meaty slabs of king oyster mushrooms make an impressive vegetable side dish. While luxurious, these mushrooms are not exotic in Taiwan, grown in farms rather than foraged in the wild. Their porous flesh has a delicate flavor that's best enjoyed with minimal seasoning, like a touch of ginger added to the oil for a simple sauté.

1 pound king oyster or king trumpet oyster mushrooms

2 tablespoons vegetable or peanut oil

1 tablespoon peeled and julienned fresh ginger

¼ teaspoon salt

Clean any dirt from the mushrooms with damp paper towels. Slice lengthwise into strips about ¼ inch thick.

Heat the oil in a large skillet or wok over medium-high heat. Add the ginger and cook until fragrant, about 10 seconds. Arrange the mushroom slices in the pan to allow as much surface contact as possible and sprinkle with the salt. Cook, without stirring, to gently brown the mushrooms, about 30 seconds. Then stir and toss around to gently brown the other sides, and cook until the mushrooms are just translucent rather than opaque white, 3 to 4 minutes more. Transfer to a serving dish and enjoy immediately.

Braised Cabbage with Dried Shrimp and Shiitake Mushrooms (Lu Bai Cai)

滷白菜

Makes 4 to 6 servings

A ubiquitous vegetable side dish at the Taiwanese table, this preparation marries the gentle sweetness of green cabbage with salty, umami-laced specks of dried baby shrimp and shiitake mushrooms. For extra color and a hint of spice, I've added a bit of chili bean sauce, which turns the generous braising liquids a vibrant gold.

1 tablespoon dried baby shrimp, soaked in ½ cup warm water for at least 10 minutes

3 to 4 dried shiitake mushrooms, soaked in 2 cups cold water until reconstituted (about 30 minutes)

2 tablespoons vegetable or peanut oil

2 garlic cloves, thinly sliced

1 pound green cabbage, coarsely shredded

Salt to taste

1 teaspoon chili bean sauce

Drain the shrimp and squeeze to remove excess liquid. Coarsely chop. Drain the mushrooms and squeeze to remove excess liquid; reserve the mushroom-soaking liquid (if there are any bits of grit in the liquid, strain it through a fine-mesh colander). Remove the tough stems and slice into thin slivers.

Heat the oil in a large skillet or wok with a lid over medium-high heat. Add the garlic and chopped shrimp and mushrooms and cook, stirring, until fragrant, about 10 seconds. Add the cabbage and a couple pinches of salt. Stir or turn the cabbage with tongs to wilt. Pour the reserved mushroom soaking liquid into the pan. Bring the liquid just to a boil, then reduce to a simmer. Stir in the chili bean sauce to distribute evenly. Cover and cook until the cabbage is very soft, 4 to 6 minutes. Taste and add salt as desired. Serve immediately.

Sautéed King Oyster Mushrooms with Ginger (page 104) / Braised Cabbage with Dried Shrimp and Shiitake Mushrooms (page 105)

Braised Eggplant with Garlic and Basil (Jiu Ceng Ta Qie Zi)

九層塔茄子

Makes about 4 servings

A little sweet, a little spicy, and very herbal, this braised eggplant dish incorporates lots of fresh basil as a signature finishing touch. Depending on your taste for heat, you can increase, decrease, or omit the chili bean sauce used in the recipe at your own discretion.

1 pound long slender Asian eggplant

1¼ cups water

¼ cup light soy sauce, or more to taste

2 teaspoons chili bean sauce, or more to taste

1 teaspoon sugar, or more to taste

3 tablespoons vegetable or peanut oil

3 to 4 garlic cloves, minced

¼ teaspoon salt, or more to taste

1 teaspoon cornstarch

¼ cup packed fresh Thai basil leaves

Trim the ends from the eggplant and slice into pieces about ½ inch thick. In a small bowl, mix 1 cup of the water, the soy sauce, chili bean sauce, and sugar.

Heat the oil in a large skillet or wok over medium-high heat and add the garlic. Cook until just fragrant, about 30 seconds, and then add the eggplant and salt. Cook, stirring, until the eggplant pieces are thoroughly coated in the oil and garlic, about 30 seconds more. Pour in the soy sauce mixture and continue to cook, stirring occasionally, until it reaches a boil. Reduce the heat to a simmer. Let simmer, uncovered, stirring or flipping the eggplant occasionally, until the eggplant pieces are very tender and no longer white in color, about 15 minutes. Taste for seasoning, adding salt, sugar, soy sauce, or chili sauce as desired.

In a small bowl, stir together the cornstarch and the remaining ¼ cup water and pour into the pan. Stir and cook until the liquid bubbles and thickens. Remove from the heat and toss in the basil. Stir to wilt the basil thoroughly and serve immediately.

Sautéed Sweet Potato Leaves with Garlic (Suan Rong Fan Shu Ye)

蒜茸番薯葉

Makes about 4 servings

The broad, thin leaves that emerge above the ground from the sweet potato plant are entirely edible and mild tasting. Sweet potatoes are a traditional source of nutrition in Taiwan, as they're easy to grow and provide more vitamins and nutrients than a bowl of rice for farmers working a long, hard day in the field. Hence, the greens are conveniently harvested for cooking as well. Their soft texture and quick cooking time is similar to spinach leaves.

2 tablespoons vegetable or peanut oil

3 garlic cloves, thinly sliced

½ pound sweet potato leaves, tough stems trimmed

Salt to taste

½ cup water

Heat the oil in a large skillet or wok over medium-high heat and add the garlic. Once fragrant and very hot, add the sweet potato leaves along with a pinch of salt and stir to wilt. Add the water, a splash at a time, to encourage wilting without burning the garlic. Cook, stirring occasionally, until completely wilted, 2 to 3 minutes, tasting for seasoning and add salt as desired. Serve immediately.

Sautéed Water Spinach with Fermented Tofu (Fu Ru Kong Xin Cai)

腐乳空心菜

Makes about 4 servings

Crisp, mild-tasting water spinach is a favorite leafy green enjoyed in Taiwan. When lightly sautéed, the hollow stalks retain a crisp texture that's appealing enough for the finest banquet tables. While often simply sautéed with garlic, a touch of fermented tofu is sometimes added to provide a hint of savory flavor and a cloudy complexion to the liquids released from the greens. Fermented tofu is found in tiny cubes packed in small jars, and is extremely stinky and potent. Only a small dab needs to be used, mixed with some water, to gently flavor an entire dish of these greens.

½ teaspoon fermented tofu

½ cup water

2 tablespoons vegetable or peanut oil

About ½ pound water spinach, tough stems trimmed and cut into 2-inch pieces

Salt to taste

Mix the fermented tofu with the water in a small bowl.

Heat the oil in a large skillet or wok over medium-high heat until very hot. Add the water spinach along with a couple pinches of salt. Cook, stirring, to wilt completely, about 2 minutes. Pour in the fermented tofu mixture and stir to incorporate thoroughly. Cook for another 1 to 2 minutes to heat through, tasting for seasoning and adding salt as desired. Serve immediately.

Dragon Beard Fern Ohitashi (Liang Ban Long Xu Cai)

涼拌龍鬚菜

Makes about 2 servings

Dragon beard fern, with its curlicue ends, is a wild green popularized by Taiwan's aboriginal communities, who harvest them from the wild. They resemble pea shoots with their twirling stems, but are actually a bit tougher and take longer to cook. Here, the greens are blanched in boiling water then shocked in an ice bath to retain their vibrant color. A slightly sweetened soy-based liquid is drenched over the dish in a typical Japanese serving method known as ohitashi.

About ½ pound dragon beard fern, tough stems trimmed

½ cup water

¼ cup light soy sauce

¼ cup rice wine

1 teaspoon sugar

Bring a pot of salted water to a boil. Prepare a large bowl of ice water and set aside. Submerge the greens in the boiling water and cook for 2 to 3 minutes. Transfer with tongs immediately to the ice bath to cool. Drain and squeeze well to remove excess liquid.

Combine the ½ cup water, soy sauce, rice wine, and sugar in a small pot and bring to a boil, stirring to dissolve the sugar. Cook for about 1 minute more. Remove from the heat and let cool for a few minutes.

Chop the drained greens into roughly 2-inch pieces and arrange on a serving dish. Pour the sauce over the greens and serve.

Stuffed Bitter Melon (Niang Ku Gua)

釀苦瓜

Makes about 4 servings

Bitter melon, or bitter gourd, is well appreciated in Taiwan for its detoxifying health benefits. There's a saying in Chinese that one must "eat bitter" before reaping sweet rewards. But its strikingly bitter taste is appreciated on its own, especially in contrast to multicourse meals with rich, heavy dishes like pork belly. Found in Asian markets, bitter melon may be pale green in color or white, and has shiny skin with a distinctive wrinkled surface. This recipe incorporates slices of the melon stuffed with a pork dumpling–style filling for attractive bite-sized pieces.

For the stuffing

½ pound ground pork

2 whole scallions, trimmed and finely chopped

1 teaspoon light soy sauce

1 teaspoon sesame oil

½ teaspoon cornstarch

¼ teaspoon salt

¼ teaspoon ground white pepper

To continue

2 medium bitter melons

1 to 2 cups hot Basic Pork Soup Stock (optional; see page 128)

For the stuffing

In a large bowl, combine the pork, scallions, soy sauce, oil, cornstarch, salt, and white pepper. You can do this up to a day ahead and store, covered, in the refrigerator.

To continue

Trim the ends from the melons and slice into rounds about ½ inch thick. Entirely scoop out the seed pockets from the centers of the slices. Bring a large pot of salted water to a boil and submerge the slices. Blanch for 2 to 3 minutes, then drain.

Arrange the melon slices on a flat plate that fits inside a steamer (or directly onto a bamboo steamer rack lined with parchment paper). Fill each center completely with a scoop of the filling mixture. Steam until the filling feels firm to the touch and is entirely cooked through, 8 to 10 minutes. Transfer carefully to a deep serving dish. If desired, ladle the stock in a shallow pool at the bottom of the dish for serving.

Stuffed Bitter Melon
(page 113)

Okra with Garlic, Chilies, and Fermented Black Beans (page 116)

Okra with Garlic, Chilies, and Fermented Black Beans (Dou Chi Chao Qiu Kui)

豆豉炒秋葵

Makes about 4 servings

Tasty and colorful, this dish infuses fresh, whole okra pods with pungent flavor. Most Taiwanese do not mind much the viscous, seeded interior of okra, but enjoy its natural textures. For those who are not so on board, this recipe can be made just as well with fresh, crisp green beans instead of okra.

2 tablespoons vegetable or peanut oil

2 garlic cloves, finely chopped

2 to 3 small fresh red chilies, finely sliced

½ pound okra pods

Salt to taste

1 tablespoon fermented black beans

¾ cup water

Heat the oil in a large skillet or wok with a lid over medium-high heat. Add the garlic and chilies and cook, stirring, just until fragrant, 1 minute. Add the okra pods along with a pinch of salt and cook, stirring occasionally, until their color just deepens, about 30 seconds. Stir in the black beans. Add the water and bring just to a boil. Cover and cook until the okra is tender, 3 to 4 minutes. (Taste the okra to test for doneness.) Season with additional salt if desired and serve immediately.

Deep-Fried Sweet Potato Balls (You Zha Di Gua Qiu)

油炸地瓜球

Makes 16 to 20 balls

Sweet potatoes are an old-fashioned treat in Taiwan. Because they're so naturally sweet, they need little seasoning or embellishment. One can usually find street vendors with a portable oven serving sweet potatoes simply roasted in their skins for snacking. This is especially fitting for the smaller, longer, and incredibly sweet-tasting varieties that are commonly grown in Taiwan (often also called yams, or Japanese yams). However, in this recipe, sweet potatoes are cooked and formed into bite-sized morsels for deep-frying until crispy and golden. Once fried, these nuggets almost resemble doughnut bites. The same batter can also be formed into balls that are then boiled until soft and chewy; these boiled pieces are often sprinkled onto crushed ice desserts (see page 232) or drizzled with sweet syrup and served chilled.

1 pound sweet potatoes, peeled and cut into 2-inch cubes

1 teaspoon sugar

1 cup sweet potato starch, or more as needed, plus more for dusting

4 cups vegetable or peanut oil, or more as needed, for frying

Prepare a steamer with boiling water underneath. Arrange the sweet potatoes in the steamer, cover, and steam until tender throughout when a fork is inserted into the center, at least 10 minutes. Transfer immediately to a large bowl and mash well with a potato masher, ricer, or spatula until smooth. Stir in the sugar until dissolved.

Working while the potato mixture is still warm, gradually stir in the sweet potato starch until fully incorporated. The mixture should resemble a puttylike dough; add slightly more starch, a little at a time, if the mixture is too wet or sticky to handle. Form the mixture into 2 balls. Turn onto a surface lightly coated with starch and roll each one into a log about 1 inch thick. Cut into 1-inch pieces.

Add the oil to a wok or pot so that it is deep enough to submerge the balls (use more oil if necessary). Heat over medium-high heat until a candy thermometer inserted into the oil (but not touching the pan) reads between 350° and 375°F. When cooking, adjust the heat if necessary to maintain this temperature. Carefully drop in the balls (about 4 at a time), working in batches to ensure the balls fry without sticking together. Fry for at least 30 seconds, then turn the balls over with chopsticks or tongs. Continue to cook until golden brown all over, another 1 to 2 minutes. Transfer immediately to paper towels. Serve immediately.

Dry Tofu with Edamame (Dou Gan Chao Mao Dou Ren)

豆干炒毛豆仁

Makes about 4 servings

This simple, home-style dish is something that my grandfather whipped up as a quick, inexpensive, yet nutritious and protein-filled meal to serve with rice. You'll need to find dry tofu (or tofu-gan) from an Asian grocery, preferably five-spice–flavored varieties that are stained tan from a long simmer in a soy sauce–based broth. Dry five-spice tofu is commonly enjoyed in Taiwan because it is great for stir-frying until slightly crisped and browned on the sides. This recipe pairs neat cubes of it with sweet green soybeans (or edamame), to match their relative size and shape.

2 cups fresh or thawed frozen shelled edamame

2 tablespoons vegetable or peanut oil

2 garlic cloves, minced

1 teaspoon peeled and minced fresh ginger

½ pound dry five-spice tofu, chopped into roughly ½-inch cubes

2 teaspoons light soy sauce, or more to taste

1 teaspoon chili bean sauce, or more to taste (optional)

Bring a small pot of lightly salted water to a boil and add the edamame. Cook until just tender, about 2 to 3 minutes, and then drain.

Heat the oil in a large skillet or wok over medium-high heat and add the garlic and ginger. Cook, stirring, until fragrant, about 1 minute. Add the tofu cubes and cook, stirring occasionally, until evenly browned on its sides, about 2 minutes. Add the edamame, soy sauce, and chili bean sauce, if using, and toss to coat evenly. Taste for seasoning, adding more soy sauce or chili bean sauce as desired. Serve immediately.

Pan-Fried Tofu with Date Sauce (Gan Mei Dou Fu)

甘梅豆腐

Makes about 4 servings

There are many sweet-and-sour sauces based on plums, dates, and other fruits. I was attracted to a dish of pan-fried tofu with date sauce on one of my most recent trips to Taiwan because it reflected this natural approach to an otherwise common sweet-and-sour sauce, with wonderful nuances of flavor. Dried dates come in many varieties in Taiwan, but the dried brown dates found in most U.S. groceries work fine to achieve this concentrated fruity flavor. It is a little time-consuming to make the sauce from scratch rather than find a jar of date or plum sauce, but well worth the effort for the natural richness of flavor.

For the sauce

1 cup dried pitted dates

1¼ cups water, or more as needed

¼ cup rice vinegar, or more to taste

¼ cup light soy sauce, or more to taste

1 teaspoon sugar, or more to taste

1 teaspoon cornstarch

To continue

¼ cup vegetable or peanut oil

1 pound extra-firm tofu, cut into ½-inch-thick rectangles

Salt to taste

For the sauce

In a small saucepan, cover the dates with 1 cup of the water (or enough water to just cover) and bring to a boil. Cover the pot, remove from the heat, and let the dates soak for at least 30 minutes or preferably 1 hour. Transfer the mixture to a blender or food processor and puree for several minutes until there are no more visible chunks. Strain through a fine-mesh colander and press through with a spatula to extract all the thick puree while removing the bits of skin.

Bring the strained date mixture just to a boil in a small saucepan. Stir in the vinegar, soy sauce, and sugar and taste for seasoning, adding additional vinegar, soy sauce, or sugar as desired.

In a small bowl, stir together the cornstarch and the remaining ¼ cup water. Stir the cornstarch mixture into the sauce. Cook until the sauce bubbles and thickens, about 30 seconds, then remove from the heat.

To continue

Heat the oil in a wide saucepan or wok over medium-high heat. Once very hot, arrange the tofu slabs in a single layer so that the undersides have full contact with the pan (you may need to work in batches). Sprinkle with salt. Cook until the undersides are lightly browned, about 1 minute, and then flip to brown the other side. If working in batches, repeat with the remaining tofu. Once all the tofu pieces are gently browned on both sides, return to the pan and toss very gently with the sauce. Serve immediately.

Stinky Tofu

For anyone who's ever been to Taiwan, you'll know the smell. You'll hear the words. And you may even try a taste. But unless you're truly from Taiwan, you might not understand the incredible allure of this classic street food snack: stinky tofu. Stinky tofu may be an acquired taste for visitors but it's quite similar in theory to the smelliest of blue cheeses. Its potent flavor is uniquely delicious, or horrendous, depending on whom you ask. In any case, it's a sensation on the taste buds that you can't quite get from anything else.

At a tofu factory

To say this delicacy is unique to Taiwan isn't quite accurate; forms of stinky tofu exist throughout Asia—for instance, as the pungent, fermented soy product natto of Japan, or as small cubes that are stirred into sauces, like in the recipe for Sautéed Water Spinach with Fermented Tofu (see page 110). But nowhere else but in Taiwan does stinky tofu hold such commonplace appeal, often served deep-fried and covered with sweet-and-sour sauce from food carts. These fried, puffy blocks of fermented tofu were some of the earliest specialties of Taiwanese street food, thanks to the novelty of their deep-fried preparation and unmistakable aroma. My mother recalls racing after the smell of a stinky tofu cart whenever it became apparent, to buy a snack before it could push on down the street. Nowadays, stinky tofu is commonly prepared in a variety of ways—steeped in a spicy Sichuan broth (ma la stinky tofu), or sliced to toss into stir-fries at the family table.

Just how does this tofu get so stinky? To make stinky tofu, blocks of tofu are simply left to ferment in an incredibly stinky brine, for sometimes only one day or up to months before being sold. The varying flavors and degrees of stinkiness are determined by the manufacturer's process, and there are vast regional differences throughout the island. Unlike the tradition of European cheeses, there are no firm production codes or recipes for making stinky tofu. Makers tend to keep their brine formulas a business secret, but in most cases, we know that the brines are made from fermented vegetables, meats, and sometimes seafood.

Legends about the invention of stinky tofu in China exist. According to common folklore, it was first made in Beijing by a failed scholar by the name of Wang Zhi He during the Qing dynasty. Needing to find another profession, he turned to making tofu. One day, he let some tofu sit for too long, and it fermented. The rest, as they say, is history.

The process of making stinky tofu is not, however, well suited to the novice. Most Taiwanese home cooks have little idea how the tofu is actually processed and fermented. Much like soy sauce, rice wine, and even blocks of tofu themselves, these foods have never held a place in the realm of average home cooking, traditionally left only to professional production facilities. In the case of stinky tofu, this is especially true, because no one would want to stink up their entire home for weeks or months to make it. Therefore, I have not included a recipe for stinky tofu in this book, although I briefly entertained the idea of its inclusion along with the pickles and sauces. Personally, I don't believe this is a feat that would be fun to experiment with at home, and given the time, smell, and mass-scale operations that it's best suited for, I don't imagine most home cooks would, either.

Fresh, stinky tofu is a rare find outside of Taiwan, making its memories all the more crave-worthy for relocated Taiwanese. Should one find some from a Chinese market, there's a recipe for the sour Vinegar-Pickled Cabbage that's commonly served alongside fried stinky tofu on page 61. And for those looking to experiment with their taste buds, just use stinky tofu in place of firm tofu in any stir-fry recipe, and experience the distinct stink.

Stinky tofu fermenting in a tofu factory

Noodles
and
Soups

Rice Noodles in Thick Soup with Pork Meatballs
(page 130)

Basic Pork Soup Stock (Tun Gu Gao Tang)

豚骨高湯

Makes about 2 quarts

Use this recipe wherever soup stock is called for in the noodle soup recipes that follow. Pork bones for soup are easily found in Chinese butcher shops, although if you're hard-pressed to find them, you can make a chicken or beef stock version using chicken backs or beef bones, instead. Due to the predominance of pork in Taiwan, soup made from pork bones is the most common.

2 tablespoons vegetable or peanut oil

1 (2-inch) piece fresh ginger, cut into thick strips

4 garlic cloves, smashed

2 to 3 whole scallions, trimmed and coarsely chopped

2 pounds pork bones for stock (see headnote)

4 quarts water

Salt to taste

Heat the oil in a heavy-bottomed soup pot or Dutch oven over medium-high heat. Add the ginger, garlic, and scallions and cook, stirring occasionally, until very fragrant, about 1 minute. Add the bones and cook, stirring, until just fragrant, about 1 minute. Add the water and bring to a boil. Skim the scum that froths to the surface while boiling for 5 minutes. Reduce the heat to a simmer and cook, uncovered, for at least 2 hours or preferably 3 hours. Strain the broth through a fine-mesh colander. Season with salt to taste.

A street vendor selling noodles

Rice Noodles in Thick Soup with Pork Meatballs (Rou Geng / Ba Kinn)

肉焿

Makes 4 to 6 servings

Clear and viscous, tinged with black vinegar, this thick soup is the basis for many iterations of rice noodle soup. It actually shares many similarities with the Chinese-American staple of hot-and-sour soup, swimming with shredded vegetables like cabbage, carrots, and bamboo shoots. Hearty and comforting, this famous version is studded with soft, springy morsels of pork covered in fishcake batter. That's right, not just meatballs, but fish-meatballs, if you will. You can swap in tender strips of chicken breast instead of pork, or just drop in fishcake batter for pure fish balls, without the meat.

For the meatballs

½ pound pork shoulder, thinly sliced

¼ teaspoon salt

¼ teaspoon ground white pepper

1 cup fishcake batter for Fried Fishcakes (see page 201)

For the soup

6 cups Basic Pork Soup Stock (see page 128)

2 cups packed shredded napa cabbage

1 cup julienned fresh bamboo shoots (see Note, page 159) or canned, rinsed well

1 cup julienned carrots

1 cup thinly sliced shiitake mushrooms (reconstituted dried mushrooms or fresh), de-stemmed

½ teaspoon ground white pepper

Salt to taste

2 teaspoons cornstarch

¼ cup cold water

1 tablespoon black rice vinegar

1 tablespoon sesame oil

To continue

1 pound rice noodles

1 small bunch coarsely chopped fresh cilantro, about 1 cup

Making pan-fried rice noodles in a home kitchen

For the meatballs

Season the pork with the salt and white pepper. Bring a small pot of water to a boil. Place about 1 teaspoon of the fishcake batter in your palm and cover it with a strip of pork. Squeeze your hand shut to form the pork into a squiggly, tubelike shape. Once all the pork strips are formed, drop them into the pot of boiling water and cook just until they float, about 2 minutes. Drain and set aside.

For the soup

Bring the stock to a boil in a large pot. Add the cabbage, bamboo shoots, carrots, mushrooms, white pepper, and salt to taste. Stir in the meatballs and reduce the heat to a simmer. Cook at a low simmer for at least 20 minutes or up to 2 hours.

Raise the heat to a steady boil. In a small bowl, stir together the cornstarch and water. Stir the cornstarch mixture into the soup and continue to cook, stirring, until the soup is slightly thickened, about 1 minute. Stir in the vinegar and oil and remove from the heat.

To continue

Cook the noodles according to the package instructions and drain. Divide the noodles among individual serving bowls. Ladle the soup into each bowl. Garnish with the cilantro, and serve immediately.

Taiwanese Beef Noodle Soup (Niu Rou Mian)

牛肉麵

Makes 6 to 8 servings

It's widely believed that this hallmark of Taiwanese cuisine was created within the military villages set up to accommodate the influx of mainlanders at the middle of the twentieth century. There is nowhere else a noodle soup quite like it, although the dish has conspicuous influences from Sichuan province—chili bean sauce and Sichuan peppercorns. Some call it Taiwan's "national dish," while others argue that Danzai Noodle Soup (see page 138) is more representative of older, more traditional Taiwanese cuisine. Regardless, its deeply savory, delicious broth has made it a popular favorite on the island, and amongst visitors, too.

2 to 3 tablespoons vegetable or peanut oil

2 pounds beef stew meat, preferably boneless shank, cut into 2-inch cubes

6 thick slices peeled fresh ginger

6 garlic cloves, smashed

2 whole scallions, trimmed and coarsely chopped

2 to 3 small fresh red chilies

1 large plum tomato, coarsely chopped

2 tablespoons sugar

1 tablespoon chili bean sauce

1 cup rice wine

½ cup light soy sauce

¼ cup dark soy sauce

2½ quarts water

1 tablespoon Sichuan peppercorns

½ teaspoon five-spice powder

2 star anise

To continue

2 pounds Asian wheat noodles (any width)

1 whole scallion, trimmed and thinly sliced

8 small heads gently blanched baby bok choy, or substitute with spinach, sweet potato leaves, or other leafy green vegetable (optional)

Heat 1 tablespoon of the oil in a large soup pot or Dutch oven over medium-high heat. Once hot, add as much of the beef as will fit on the bottom of the pan without too much overlap (you will need to work in batches). Cook, flipping with tongs, until both sides are gently browned, 5 to 6 minutes total. Repeat with the remaining beef, adding more oil as needed. Transfer the meat to a dish and set aside.

Heat another tablespoon of the oil in the same pot until just hot. Add the ginger, garlic, scallions, chilies, and tomato. Cook, stirring occasionally, until very fragrant and the vegetables are softened, 3 to 4 minutes. Stir in the sugar and cook until dissolved and the mixture is bubbling. Return the beef to the pan and stir in the chili bean sauce.

Stir in the rice wine and bring to a boil, scraping the bottom of the pot to release any browned bits. Let boil for a minute, then add the light and dark soy sauces, the water, peppercorns, five-spice powder, and star anise. Bring just to a boil and then reduce to a low simmer. Skim the scum that rises to the top of the pot with a slotted spoon. Cover and cook at a low simmer for at least 2 hours, preferably 3 hours.

To continue
Cook the noodles according to the package instructions. Divide among individual serving bowls. Ladle the soup into each bowl with chunks of the beef, top with scallions and the blanched green vegetables, if using, and serve.

Military Villages (Juan Cun) and Food

When the Republic of China relocated to Taiwan in 1947–1949, they were not thinking of long-term settlement. They needed to house the Kuomintang army and their families, and they quickly built small, efficient housing villages (or juan cun) on public land throughout cities in Taiwan. With little funding for the immense scope of the building project, these villages were cramped and haphazardly constructed—with a shared courtyard and tiny quarters to each family. Insulated from the rest of Taiwan's society, these mainland Chinese enclaves stood testament to the divide between the two cultures. But within each village, it was a melting pot of its own—of various mainland Chinese backgrounds, who brought with them their own food cultures.

The communal atmosphere of juan cun fostered the development of many mainland-inspired foods that became favorites on the island—like beef noodle soup (page 132), with its hearty, Sichuan spice–accented broth, or red-braised pork belly-stuffed gua bao (page 67). Many more such wheat-based noodles, buns, and dumplings have been reinvented or given a new flair in Taiwan. In general, the use of wheat in Taiwanese cuisine is attributed to the arrival of mainland Chinese from this period. Before, noodles in Taiwan were typically made of rice flour and there were few dumplings or buns, with the exception of glutinous, rice starch–based ones, like ba-wan (page 91). Because it was efficient to cook for several families at once, regional styles mixed and mingled frequently in these villages.

It didn't take long for the food traditions of mainland China to trickle into Taiwanese cuisine. As the years went by, many former ROC soldiers went into culinary businesses to make ends meet. This propelled the popularity of such mainland-inspired foods throughout Taiwan. Now, snacking on guotie (page 73) and steamed buns is prevalent throughout the island, and wheat noodles are often employed in traditional Taiwanese dishes, like Danzai Noodle Soup (page 138). Shanghai-style soup dumplings have become a national obsession as well. (The founder of Din Tai Fun, Taiwan's landmark Michelin-starred restaurant, which specializes in soup dumplings, was a mainland Chinese man who moved to Taiwan in 1948.) Beef noodle soup, believed to have been born within juan cun walls, is often lauded as the national dish of the island.

It's interesting to note the many contributions to what we now know of as Taiwanese cuisine from this mass-scale mainland arrival. Just as the Japanese had done during its occupation, this comparably smaller group of people would influence the food of Taiwan in lasting ways. But it's also important to understand how much juan cun, and its resulting food traditions,

represented an unfair segmentation of society. For all their cramped conditions and communal meals by necessity, military families did not pay for their housing, as the villages were owned by the government. They were also rationed basic provisions like rice and flour in the early days. Over the years, the buildings received updates, such as electricity and modern plumbing, as the residents continued to live there long after the last activities of the war with the Communists. These advantages further set them apart from the Taiwanese people who had lived on the island for generations. The uncertainty of whether the war with the Communists would continue left many members of the military—and their dependents—confused about their place in society. With little experience and education, it's not surprising that many of them turned to food businesses.

Today, some Taiwanese would argue against beef noodle soup as its true national dish since it's a relic of the mainland Chinese food imposed upon the Taiwanese food eaten before this period on the island. Similarly, they would argue that restaurants specializing in mainland cuisine like Din Tai Fung are not the best representation of Taiwan's unique food culture. This is understandable, and responsible for a growing interest in more traditional snacks and dishes from Taiwan. Yet more so than strictly adhering to Chinese recipes, the mainland arrival paved the way for innovation, and a blending of food styles around the island. For instance, Taiwanese beef noodle soup is not found in Sichuan province, or elsewhere in China. This is perhaps owed in large part to juan cun living. (My mother's family lived in one for most of her childhood in Taipei. My relatives also recall that every other every street food vendor in the city was an aging former ROC soldier.)

Today, most of the eight-hundred-plus juan cun villages have been demolished to make room for high-rise condos or more stable, up-to-date buildings. There

Soup dumplings at Taiwan's reowned Din Tai Fung restaurant

A steamed basket of soup dumplings

have been efforts to preserve the ones still standing as historic monuments. Whether or not that is achieved, there can be no denying that the food legacies from its era have been well preserved. The fact that so many of this mainland generation turned to food and found moderate success in this area serves as an interesting piece of Taiwan's culinary evolution. In addition, it shows how food was one of the first ways of bridging the gaps between the conflicting groups on the island. This tradition continues, and thanks to Taiwan's adventurous appetite, influences from around the world can be found in Taiwanese food.

Danzai Noodle Soup (Dan Zai Mian)

擔仔麵

Makes 6 servings

This noodle soup was originally created by fishermen during the off-season (or slack season) for their catch. These fishermen and erstwhile food peddlers would carry their noodles in one bucket and their soup and other ingredients in another, hanging from opposite ends of a pole placed on the back of their shoulders. ("Danzai" refers to the wooden pole.) While simple—composed of a single shrimp placed atop a scoop of hearty minced pork sauce—the noodle soup is so well loved in Taiwan that restaurant chains have been focused on the dish, enjoying decades of success. Some chefs like to place a small mound of freshly grated garlic underneath the shrimp. It seems like this might have originally served to mask any off flavors of not-so-fresh shrimp, but it's a distinct touch in any case.

For the soup

6 large shrimp with heads and shells on

6 cups Basic Pork Soup Stock (see page 128)

To continue

1 pound Asian egg noodles (chow mein)

1 cup Pork Meat Sauce (see page 180)

2 garlic cloves, grated

¼ cup black vinegar

2 whole scallions, trimmed and finely chopped

For the soup

Peel the shrimp except for the tip of the tails. Remove the heads and devein the shrimp. Retain the heads and shells and place in a pot. Cover with the stock. Bring to a boil and then reduce the heat to a simmer. Cook at a simmer, uncovered, for about 30 minutes. Strain the soup and discard the shells. Return the soup to a clean pot and bring just to a boil again. Drop in the shrimp and blanch until firm, opaque, and fully cooked, about 2 minutes (depending on size). Transfer from the soup with a slotted spoon and set aside.

To continue

Cook the noodles according to the package instructions and drain. Warm the pork sauce in a separate pot. Divide the noodles among 6 serving bowls. Ladle in the hot broth. Top each bowl of noodles with a spoonful of the pork sauce, about half a teaspoon of the garlic, and 1 shrimp. Drizzle the black vinegar atop each bowl. Sprinkle the bowl with the scallions and serve immediately.

Oyster Noodle Soup
(E Zai Mian Xian / O Ah Mi Suan)
蚵仔麵線
Makes 4 to 6 servings

Slurrp. This dish is popular curbside cuisine in southern Taiwan counties, especially coastal cities where oysters are caught nearby. Its popularity has spurred restaurants and night market stalls throughout the island, and at many shops, boiled pork intestines may be served atop the noodles in addition to oysters. The type of noodles used are thin wheat flour noodles cut short, stirred directly into the soup for added viscosity. Look for fresh (not dried) wheat noodles in an Asian grocery's refrigerator aisle for best results.

For the soup

6 cups Basic Pork Soup Stock (see page 128)

½ cup packed bonito flakes (found in Asian groceries)

¼ cup vegetable or peanut oil

6 garlic cloves, minced

2 tablespoons Fried Shallots (see page 52)

1 tablespoon sugar

1 tablespoon light soy sauce

¼ teaspoon ground white pepper

Salt to taste

1 tablespoon cornstarch

½ cup cold water

1 pound very thin fresh wheat noodles (mi sua), cut into 3- to 4-inch pieces

16 to 24 raw oysters, about 1 lb, preshucked or shucked at home

¼ cup black rice vinegar, plus extra for serving

1 tablespoon sesame oil

For serving

1 small bunch coarsely chopped fresh cilantro, about 1 cup

For the soup

In a large pot, bring the stock just to a boil, then remove from the heat. Add the bonito flakes and let soak for 10 minutes. Strain the broth through a fine-mesh colander and set aside.

Heat the vegetable oil in a skillet or wok over low heat. Add the garlic and stir. Cook until the garlic is softened and a golden or caramel color, 6 to 8 minutes (reduce the heat if the garlic begins to burn or turn darker brown). Remove from the heat and stir in the fried shallots. Transfer to a small bowl and set aside.

Pour the strained soup into a clean soup pot and bring to a boil. Add the sugar, soy sauce, white pepper, and salt to taste. In a small bowl, stir together the cornstarch and water. Stir the cornstarch mixture into the soup and continue to cook, stirring, until the soup is slightly thickened, about 1 minute. Drop in the noodles and cook directly in the soup, stirring, until the noodles are tender, at least 3 minutes. Drop in the oysters and cook for 1 to 2 more minutes. Remove from the heat and stir in the vinegar and sesame oil.

For serving

Divide the soup among 4 to 6 serving bowls. Top each bowl with a small scoop of the golden fried garlic and shallot mixture, cilantro, and a drizzle of extra black vinegar if desired.

A street vendor frying oyster fritters

Assembling a noodle soup with oysters / Aboriginal chef Chen Yao-Zhong of Claypot Lily Spring restaurant tries crab sashimi

Spanish Mackerel Noodle Soup (Tu Tun Yu Geng Mian)

土屯魚羹麵

Makes 4 to 6 servings

Oily, flavorful, darker-fleshed fish like mackerel are greatly enjoyed when in season in Taiwan. These fish need to be served as fresh as possible, due to their shorter expiration, so they're often served very minimally, as in this clear, herb-sprinkled soup in which they're delicately poached. With or without noodles, it's hearty yet simple fare.

1½ pounds Spanish mackerel fillets

2 tablespoons rice wine

Salt to taste

¼ teaspoon ground white pepper, or more to taste

6 cups Basic Pork Soup Stock (see page 128)

To continue

1 pound rice noodles

2 to 3 whole scallions, trimmed and finely chopped

2 tablespoons Fried Shallots (see page 52)

Ground white pepper (optional)

Cut the fish fillets lengthwise into roughly 1 by 2-inch slices. In a shallow dish, marinate the pieces with the rice wine, a generous pinch of salt, and the white pepper. Cover and refrigerate at least 20 minutes (or up to 2 hours).

Bring the stock to a boil in a large soup pot. Drop in the mackerel pieces. Once a piece floats to the top, remove it with a slotted spoon and transfer to a dish. Once all the pieces have cooked, skim off any scum that has risen to the top of the soup with a fine-mesh strainer. Season the soup with salt and white pepper to taste.

To continue

Cook the noodles according to the package instructions. Drain and divide among 4 to 6 serving bowls. Ladle the soup into each bowl and divide the mackerel pieces. Top each bowl with the scallions, fried shallots, and a sprinkle of white pepper, if desired.

Fried Pork Chop Noodle Soup (Pai Gu Mian)

排骨麵

Makes 4 servings

Pounded thin and marinated overnight, Taiwanese pork chop cutlets are always juicy and flavorful. These crispy, fried pork chops are the main entrée of many on-the-go meals, often served atop a mound of plain rice alongside sautéed greens or a few pickled vegetables for tangy contrast. Served with a simple noodle soup instead, one can dip their pork chop into the soup as they alternate between bites. It's a fun meal that kids and adults both treasure.

For the pork chops

4 bone-in pork chops (about ¼ pound each)

2 tablespoons light soy sauce

4 garlic cloves, grated

1 tablespoon sugar

1 teaspoon five-spice powder

½ teaspoon salt

½ teaspoon ground white pepper

1 tablespoon sesame oil

3 to 4 cups vegetable or peanut oil, or more as needed, for frying

4 large eggs, lightly beaten

½ cup water

1 cup sweet potato starch

For the soup

6 cups Basic Pork Soup Stock (see page 128)

Salt and white pepper to taste

To continue

1 pound wheat or rice noodles

Fresh chopped scallions (optional)

Pickled Mustard Greens (optional; see page 57)

Tea Eggs (optional; see page 85)

For the pork chops

Place the pork chops one at a time on a cutting board and cover with a layer of plastic wrap. Pound with a meat pounder, avoiding the bone, until the chop is no thicker than ¼ inch. Rub each pounded pork chop with the soy sauce, garlic, sugar, five-spice powder, salt, white pepper, and sesame oil. Cover and refrigerate at least 2 hours (preferably overnight, or up to 1 day ahead).

Add the vegetable oil to a saucepan or wok that is deep enough to completely submerge the pork chops (use more oil if necessary). Heat over medium-high heat until a candy thermometer inserted into the oil (but not touching the pan) reads between 350° to 375°F. Combine the eggs with the water in a bowl and place beside a bowl of the sweet potato starch. Dip each pork chop into the egg wash to coat thoroughly, followed by the starch to coat thoroughly. Shake off any excess starch. Carefully lower a pork chop into the oil. Fry until very golden-brown on one side, 2 to 3 minutes, then carefully flip and fry to brown the opposite side, about 2 minutes more. Transfer with tongs to paper towels immediately and repeat with the rest of the chops.

For the soup

Bring the stock to a boil in a large soup pot. Season the soup with salt and white pepper to taste.

To continue

Cook the noodles according to the package instructions. Drain and divide among 4 serving bowls. Ladle the hot soup into each bowl. For ease of eating, the pork chops may be cut into long strips to serve alongside or on top of the noodle soup.

For the optional garnish and side dishes: Garnish with the scallions and serve with the pickled mustard greens and tea eggs on the side, if desired.

Pan-Fried Egg Noodles with Seafood (Hai Xian Chao Mian)

海鮮炒麵

Makes 4 to 6 servings

In coastal cities where fishing boats are docked, one can often find seafood markets with built-in eateries beneath tents in Taiwan. Here, seafood is served up as fresh as it gets, and no matter what the type of fish, shellfish, or crustacean, one popular way to serve it is simply sautéed with typical Taiwanese herbs and spices. This pan-fried noodle dish features an assortment of seafood with a hint of sha-cha sauce, fresh chilies, and Thai basil. Don't be afraid to add or subtract any of the types of seafood called for in the recipe in keeping with the spirit—go with whatever looks the freshest at your market.

1 pound Asian egg noodles (chow mein)

¼ cup vegetable or peanut oil

1 tablespoon peeled and julienned fresh ginger

4 garlic cloves, minced

4 to 6 small fresh red chilies, coarsely chopped

½ pound whole shrimp, peeled and deveined

Salt to taste

½ pound cleaned squid, sliced into rings and tentacles kept intact

1 cup rice wine

¼ cup light soy sauce, or more to taste

1 tablespoon sugar

2 teaspoons Sha-Cha Sauce (see page 53)

1 dozen manila clams, rinsed and scrubbed

2 whole scallions, trimmed and coarsely chopped

1 cup packed fresh Thai basil leaves

Cook the noodles according to the package instructions. Drain and set aside.

Heat 2 tablespoons of the oil in a large skillet or wok over medium-high heat. Add the ginger, garlic, and chilies and cook, stirring occasionally, until fragrant and the oil is very hot, about 10 seconds. Add the shrimp and a pinch of salt and cook, stirring briskly, until just cooked through and no longer translucent, 1 to 2 minutes (depending on size). Remove from the pan and transfer to a dish. Add the squid to the same pan along with a pinch of salt and cook, stirring briskly, until just barely cooked and opaque, about 1 minute. Remove from the pan and set aside with the shrimp.

Add the rice wine, soy sauce, sugar, and sha-cha sauce to the same pan and bring to a boil, stirring to mix thoroughly. Once boiling, add the clams and cover the pan. After 2 to 3 minutes, peek inside to see if all the clams have opened. If necessary, continue to cook, covered, until all or most of the clams have opened, 1 to 2 minutes longer. Remove and discard any clams that have not opened after 5 minutes.

Return the shrimp and squid to the pan and stir in the noodles and scallions. Turn and toss with tongs to coat the noodles thoroughly. Taste and add salt or extra soy sauce if desired. Remove from the heat and toss the noodles once more with the basil leaves. Serve immediately.

A fishing dock with a Taoist temple nearby

Crispy Spareribs Soup with Winter Melon (Pai Gu Su Tang)

排骨酥湯

Makes 4 to 6 servings

Deep-fried nuggets of tender spareribs are paired with refreshing cubes of winter melon in this delightful soup. The Taiwanese enjoy soaking these crispy, fried chunks of ribs completely in the soup before nibbling away at them, much like fried-then-soaked fish cakes. Winter melon, a white, crisp, and neutral-tasting melon found in Asian groceries, becomes translucent and melt-in-your-mouth tender when added to soups. As an alternative, you could chop daikon radish into cubes instead of winter melon.

For the spareribs

1 pound bone-in spareribs, sliced by the butcher into 1- to 2-inch-long sections

2 teaspoons light soy sauce

1 teaspoon sesame oil

1 teaspoon cornstarch

2 garlic cloves, grated

½ teaspoon sugar

¼ teaspoon five-spice powder

¼ teaspoon salt

¼ teaspoon ground white pepper

3 to 4 cups vegetable or peanut oil, or more as needed, for frying

2 large eggs, lightly beaten

¼ cup water

½ cup sweet potato starch

For the soup

6 cups Basic Pork Soup Stock (see page 128)

½ pound winter melon, cut into ½-inch cubes

Salt and ground white pepper to taste

To continue

1 pound rice noodles

1 small bunch coarsely chopped fresh cilantro, about 1 cup

Fried Shallots (see page 52)

For the spareribs

In a bowl, marinate the spareribs with the soy sauce, sesame oil, cornstarch, garlic, sugar, five-spice powder, salt, and white pepper. Cover and refrigerate for at least 20 minutes (or up to 1 day).

Prepare a steamer or double boiler with plenty of boiling water underneath. Arrange the spareribs on a plate and set inside the steamer. Cover and steam until the pieces are tender to the touch, 35 to 45 minutes. Let cool completely.

Add the oil to a saucepan or wok that is deep enough to submerge the sparerib pieces (use more oil if necessary). Heat over medium-high heat until a candy thermometer inserted into the oil (but not touching the pan) reads between 350° to 375°F. In a small bowl, combine the eggs with the water and place beside a bowl of the sweet potato starch. Dip each sparerib piece into the egg wash, followed by the starch to coat thoroughly. Shake off any excess starch. Drop the ribs into the hot oil in batches of 4 to 5 at a time, so they fry without touching each other. Fry the pieces until golden brown all over, flipping carefully with tongs, about 2 minutes. Transfer with tongs to paper towels immediately.

For the soup

Bring the stock to a boil in a large soup pot. Drop in the winter melon cubes and return to a boil. Reduce to a simmer and cook, covered, until all the cubes are translucent and soft, 20 to 30 minutes. Season the soup with salt and white pepper to taste.

To continue

Cook the rice noodles according to the package instructions. Drain and divide among 4 to 6 serving bowls. Ladle the winter melon soup into each bowl. Divide the fried sparerib pieces among the bowls and top each one with cilantro and the fried shallots to serve.

Drying rice noodles on the roof in Hsinchu

Pan-Fried Rice Noodles with Pork and Vegetables (Chao Mi Fen)

炒米粉

Makes 4 to 6 servings

In the city of Hsinchu, in the northwest of Taiwan, the air is much windier and drier. It's where many rice noodle factories are located, as the climate allows the freshly made noodles to dry quickly. Taiwanese rice noodles are often labeled "Hsinchu rice noodles" on packages found in groceries, even in the U.S., and are exceptionally thin. One of their most famous preparations is a steaming platter of pan-fried rice noodles served at the family table for everyday and special occasions. While delicate, these rice noodles can stand up surprisingly well to a lot of tossing and turning on the pan, without breaking or sticking as easily as wheat noodles would.

½ pound pork shoulder, thinly sliced

¼ cup plus 1 teaspoon light soy sauce

½ teaspoon cornstarch

½ teaspoon sugar

¼ cup dried baby shrimp (optional)

1 pound rice noodles

3 tablespoons vegetable or peanut oil

8 to 10 dried shiitake mushrooms, soaked in 3 cups cold water until fully reconstituted (about 30 minutes), de-stemmed and thinly sliced

1 cup julienned carrots

1 cup peeled and julienned fresh bamboo shoots (see Note, page 159) or canned, rinsed well

1 cup bean sprouts (optional)

Salt and ground white pepper to taste

2 cups Basic Pork Soup Stock (see page 128)

2 tablespoons black rice vinegar

2 to 3 whole scallions, trimmed and thinly sliced

In a shallow dish, marinate the sliced pork in 1 teaspoon of the soy sauce, the cornstarch, and sugar. Cover and refrigerate for at least 20 minutes (or up to 1 day).

Soak the dried shrimp in warm water to cover for 5 to 10 minutes. Drain.

Cook the rice noodles according to the package instructions. Drain completely.

Heat the oil in a large skillet or wok over medium-high heat. Add the dried shrimp and cook for 30 seconds, stirring occasionally. Add the pork and cook, stirring frequently, until all the pieces are mostly opaque, 1 to 2 minutes. Add the mushrooms, carrots, bamboo shoots, and optional bean sprouts to the pan along with a pinch of salt. Cook, stirring occasionally, another 1 to 2 minutes. Add the stock and the remaining ¼ cup soy sauce to the pan and bring just to a boil. Drop in the cooked rice noodles and stir briskly, tossing and turning the noodles with tongs or a spatula. Season with salt and white pepper to taste. Allow the noodles to fully absorb the broth so that there's no liquid in the pan. Finally, stir in the vinegar and toss to distribute evenly. Transfer to a serving dish and garnish with the scallions.

Noodles with Minced Pork and Fermented Bean Sauce (Zha Jiang Mian)

炸醬麵

Makes 4 to 6 servings

This lukewarm, tossed noodle dish originates from Beijing, but in Taiwan, it's become quite a favorite with a few spins of its own. There's a conspicuous drizzle of black rice vinegar in many Taiwanese-prepared renditions, plenty of fresh garlic flavor, and toppings that may include green soybeans (edamame), blanched green vegetables, and crisp bean sprouts. The quintessential condiment used to prepare the sauce is a slightly sweet, fermented bean paste called tienmianjiang. Look for it in jars labeled "sweet bean sauce" at Asian supermarkets; if not to be found, the spicier chili bean sauce (see page 43) may be substituted in its place. Just go easier on the sauce in that event, unless you don't mind it very spicy.

For the sauce

1 tablespoon vegetable or peanut oil

½ pound ground pork

¼ teaspoon salt

1 tablespoon Fried Shallots (see page 52)

4 garlic cloves, minced

1 tablespoon sugar

½ cup sweet bean sauce (tienmianjiang)

2 teaspoons cornstarch

1 cup water

1 to 2 teaspoons light soy sauce, to taste

To continue

1 pound wheat noodles (any width)

½ cup fresh or thawed frozen shelled edamame

2 cups packed bok choy or napa cabbage leaves

For serving

¼ cup black rice vinegar

1 cup fresh bean sprouts

1 cup peeled and julienned cucumbers

1 cup fresh cilantro sprigs

For the sauce

Heat the oil in a skillet or wok over medium-high heat and add the pork. Sprinkle with the salt and stir-fry, breaking up the pieces, until the pork is no longer pinkish, about 1 minute. Add the fried shallots, garlic, and sugar and stir to incorporate thoroughly. Stir in the sweet bean sauce. In a separate bowl, stir together the cornstarch and water. Once the pork mixture is hot and bubbling, pour in the cornstarch mixture and continue to cook, stirring, until the mixture thickens, about 10 seconds. Taste for seasoning and add the soy sauce as desired. Remove from the heat.

To continue

Cook the noodles according to the package instructions. Drain and rinse under cold water until cool. Toss the noodles to shake off excess water.

Bring a small pot of lightly salted water to a boil. Prepare a bowl with ice water and set aside. Drop in the edamame and cook until tender, 3 to 4 minutes. Remove with a slotted spoon and set aside. Drop in the bok choy or cabbage and blanch for another 30 seconds or up to 1 minute. Remove and transfer immediately to the ice bath to cool. Once just cooled, squeeze to remove excess liquid and then shred.

For serving

Arrange the noodles in a deep, large serving bowl. Drizzle the vinegar all around. Ladle the pork sauce all across the noodles. Top with the shredded greens, edamame, bean sprouts, cucumbers, and cilantro. Toss the noodles with the sauce and toppings at the table to serve.

Sesame-Scented Thin Noodles (Ma You Mian Xian)

麻油麵線

Makes 4 to 6 servings

As rustic and simple as it gets, this soul-soothing dish might just be the cacio e pepe (pasta tossed with just cheese and black pepper) of Taiwan. Ultra-fine wheat noodles are principally used in this brothless yet warm bowl of noodles, which take on the flavors of sesame oil infused with plenty of spicy ginger root.

1 cup sesame oil

1 (2-inch) piece fresh ginger, sliced into 10 to 12 discs

1 pound very thin Asian wheat noodles

2 tablespoons Fried Shallots (see page 52)

In a small saucepan, heat the oil over medium heat for 2 to 3 minutes, or until a piece of ginger sizzles a little when dropped in. Drop in all of the ginger and cook, stirring occasionally, 3 to 4 minutes; reduce the heat if necessary to prevent the ginger from burning. Remove the pan from the heat. Carefully remove the ginger with tongs and discard.

Cook the noodles according to the package instructions and drain.

Toss the noodles thoroughly with the warm oil to coat. Divide among 4 to 6 serving bowls and top with the fried shallots.

Chilled Noodles with Chicken and Sesame Sauce(Liang Mian)

涼麵

Makes 4 to 6 servings

During Taiwan's very hot summer months, a simple meal of chilled noodles is most refreshing. Conveniently, packed boxes of these can be found in every convenience store, and versions served up elsewhere can be much more elaborate than the requisite chilled noodles, sesame sauce, and some julienned cucumber. For a more filling meal, this noodle salad often comprises strips of ham or scrambled egg; I like versions made with pale, tender slivers of chicken breast and plenty of fresh herbs.

For the chicken

½ pound chicken breast meat, sliced to thin slivers

½ teaspoon cornstarch

¼ teaspoon salt

¼ teaspoon ground white pepper

For the sauce

½ cup Asian sesame paste

¼ cup light soy sauce

¼ cup rice vinegar

¼ cup sugar

¼ cup water

2 garlic cloves, grated

2 tablespoons sesame oil

To continue

1 pound wheat noodles or Asian egg noodles (chow mein)

2 cups peeled and julienned cucumbers

1 cup julienned carrots

1 cup fresh bean sprouts

½ cup packed thinly sliced scallions

1 cup packed fresh cilantro sprigs

For the chicken

In a large bowl or dish, mix the chicken with the cornstarch, salt, and white pepper. Bring a pot of water to a boil, and drop in the chicken. Once the pieces rise to the surface, remove them from the water and transfer to a plate to cool.

For the sauce

In a bowl, whisk together the sesame paste, soy sauce, vinegar, sugar, water, garlic, and oil until completely smooth.

To continue

Cook the noodles according to the package instructions. Drain and rinse under cold water until cool. Toss and shake out the excess water.

To serve the noodles family-style, arrange the noodles in a large serving bowl. Cover with the sauce, and scatter the chicken, cucumbers, carrots, bean sprouts, scallions, and cilantro on top. Toss at the table to serve.

Note

Asian sesame paste is dense and dark tan or brown in color, because the seeds are roasted before blending, unlike tahini, which is made with raw sesame seeds. Because of its deeper flavor, it is more similar in taste to peanut butter, which may be used as a substitute if Asian sesame paste is not to be found.

Clam and Daikon Radish Soup (Ge Li Luo Buo Tang)

蛤蜊蘿蔔湯

Makes 6 to 8 servings

This simple yet elegant soup is a great way to open the palate for a multicourse meal. Light, clear, and delicate tasting, it's wonderfully quick and easy to cook, if you have broth on hand to spare.

6 cups Basic Pork Soup Stock (see page 128)

1 pound daikon radish, peeled and cut into ½-inch cubes

2 dozen manila clams, rinsed and scrubbed

Salt and ground white pepper to taste

2 tablespoons peeled and very thinly julienned fresh ginger

Bring the stock to a boil in a large soup pot. Add the daikon radish and return to a boil. Reduce the heat to a low simmer and cover. Cook until the radish cubes are very tender and translucent white throughout, 20 to 25 minutes. Raise the heat to return to a boil and drop in the clams. Let cook for 3 to 4 minutes and peek inside. Once all the clams are fully opened (discard any that do not open after 5 minutes of boiling), taste for seasoning, adding salt and white pepper to taste. Divide the soup among 6 to 8 serving bowls and sprinkle each bowl with the ginger. Serve immediately.

Chicken Soup with Bamboo Shoots and Mushrooms (Zhu Sun Ji Tang)

竹筍雞湯

Makes 6 to 8 servings

Fresh and natural bamboo shoots taste very different from the canned, pickled, heavily seasoned, and otherwise processed kinds often found in Asian cuisines. These are prized delicacies in Taiwan, where they must be harvested early in the morning, typically following a rain, so that the shoots are still less than one foot in height. These young tips of bamboo can be found in most Asian produce markets, and look like the horns of a bull. Their light, earthy flavor complements that of mushrooms, as in this clear, delicate chicken soup.

¼ cup vegetable or peanut oil

1 (2-inch) piece fresh ginger, peeled and sliced into 8 to 10 thick discs

2 pounds bone-in chicken pieces, preferably chopped by a butcher into bite-size pieces, or halved wings and drumsticks

4 quarts water

10 to 12 dried shiitake mushrooms

1 pound fresh bamboo shoots, trimmed of brown skins and tough base and sliced on the bias into long slivers

Salt and ground white pepper to taste

Heat the oil in a large soup pot or Dutch oven over medium heat. Add the ginger and cook, stirring occasionally, until sizzling and fragrant, about 30 seconds. Add the chicken pieces and cook, stirring occasionally, until gently browned in parts, 3 to 4 minutes (the chicken does not need to be fully cooked at this point).

Add the water and scrape the bottom of the pan to release any browned bits. Raise the heat to high and bring the water to a boil. Let boil, uncovered, for about 20 minutes. Skim the scum that rises to the top of the pot. Drop in the mushrooms and the bamboo shoots. Reduce the heat to a low simmer and cook, uncovered, for at least 45 minutes or up to 2 hours. Add salt and white pepper to taste and serve.

Note

To prepare fresh bamboo shoots, trim the rough, brown skins and the toughest part of the base. The resulting flesh should be tender enough to taste raw and give with only a gentle snap, rather than thick and fibrous. (Think of it as a larger, woodier asparagus.)

Thick Soup with Squid (You Yu Geng)

魷魚羹

Makes 4 to 6 servings

Fresh, tender squid is the star of this simply prepared soup. So packed with the pale-colored rings and tentacles, this dish is actually something in between a thick soup and a very saucy stir-fry. There's often a pale, minimal counterpart to many rich, heavily flavored, red-tinged dishes in Taiwan—the yin to its opposite's yang. For instance, this dish's evil twin might be Three Cup Squid (see page 212), with its heaps of herbs and sauces. Any multicourse meal should employ both types of dishes in harmony.

1 pound cleaned baby squid, sliced into thin rings and tentacles kept intact

1 tablespoon cornstarch

1 tablespoon rice wine

½ teaspoon sugar

¼ teaspoon salt, plus more to taste

¼ teaspoon ground white pepper, plus more to taste

2 tablespoons vegetable or peanut oil

1 tablespoon peeled and julienned fresh ginger

4 cups Basic Pork Soup Stock (see page 128)

2 teaspoons cornstarch

½ cup cold water

1 tablespoon finely chopped Chinese celery (or substitute with common celery, sliced thinly on a bias)

½ cup packed fresh cilantro sprigs

2 tablespoons Fried Shallots (see page 52)

In a large bowl, combine the squid with the cornstarch, rice wine, sugar, salt, and white pepper. Cover and refrigerate at least 20 minutes (or up to 4 hours).

Heat the oil in a large saucepan or wok over medium heat and add the ginger. Once the ginger is fragrant and just beginning to sizzle, add the squid and cook, tossing gently, until all the pieces have just turned opaque, about 30 seconds. Transfer to a bowl and set aside.

Add the stock to the same pan and bring just to a boil. Season with salt and white pepper to taste. In a separate bowl, stir together the cornstarch and water. Stir the cornstarch slurry into the soup and continue to cook, stirring, until the soup thickens slightly, about 30 seconds. Return the squid to the soup and stir to warm through completely.

Divide the soup among 4 to 6 serving bowls. Sprinkle each bowl with the celery, cilantro, fried shallots, and a dusting of white pepper, if desired, and serve immediately.

Chicken, Pineapple, and Bitter Melon Soup (Ku Gua Feng Li Ji Tang)

苦瓜鳳梨雞湯

Makes 8 to 10 servings

This nourishing soup is thought to be the perfect fix for when you have a cold. Sweet chunks of pineapple help soften the bitterness of the melon, and provide exciting contrast with every bite. Both these plants grow plentifully in Taiwan, and it need not be treated as medicine if you're a fan of their flavors.

1 pineapple

1 large bitter melon (white or green)

¼ cup vegetable or peanut oil

1 (2-inch) piece fresh ginger, peeled and sliced into 8 to 10 thick discs

2 pounds bone-in chicken pieces, preferably chopped by a butcher into bite-size pieces, or use halved wings and drumsticks

4 quarts water

Salt and ground white pepper to taste

Trim the fronds and base from the pineapple and cut off the tough skin. Chop lengthwise into halves and then quarters. Cut the thick center core from each quarter. Chop the remaining flesh into roughly 1-inch squares.

Cut the bitter melon into halves lengthwise. Scrape out the seed pocket on both halves with a spoon. Chop the remaining flesh into half-rings no wider than 1 inch.

Heat the oil in a large soup pot or Dutch oven over medium heat. Add the ginger and cook, stirring occasionally, until sizzling and fragrant, about 30 seconds. Add the chicken pieces and cook, stirring occasionally, until gently browned in parts, 3 to 4 minutes (the chicken does not need to be fully cooked at this point).

Add the water and scrape the bottom of the pan to release any browned bits. Raise the heat to high and bring the water to a boil. Let boil, uncovered, for about 20 minutes. Skim the scum that rises to the top of the pot. Drop in the pineapple and bitter melon. Reduce the heat to a low simmer and cook, uncovered, for at least 1½ hours, preferably 2 to 3 hours. Season with salt and white pepper to taste and serve.

Sweet Potato Congee
(Di Gua Xi Fan)
地瓜稀飯

Makes 4 to 6 servings

This old-fashioned porridge was a typical working peasant's meal in Taiwan. Sweet potatoes, with their plentiful vitamins and carbohydrates, provide more lasting nourishment and energy than most vegetables. So when meat and seafood were scarce, this humble meal could satisfy for long hours of work. Congee, or rice porridges, are made in two different ways in Taiwan: with leftover steamed rice that's reheated in water to make a thin, rice-studded soup, or by cooking the dry rice grains with plenty of water to create a souplike consistency. This recipe calls for the latter preparation. Although it's just as plain as the peasants of simpler times would have enjoyed it, this dish has become so endeared in Taiwan that it's often served in restaurants today just like this, in true nostalgic tradition.

1 cup short-grain white rice
(do not substitute long-grain or brown rice)

10 cups water

2 pounds sweet potatoes, peeled
and cut into 1-inch cubes

Combine the rice and water in a large pot and bring to a boil. Reduce the heat to a low simmer and cook, uncovered, for about 30 minutes, stirring occasionally. Add the sweet potato and continue to cook, uncovered, stirring occasionally, for about 1 more hour. Toward the last 20 minutes of cooking, stir more frequently, making sure nothing is sticking to the bottom of the pot. Remove from the heat as soon as the congee is the consistency of a thickened soup and ladle into bowls for serving.

Meat
and
Poultry

Pork Meat Sauce over Rice (page 180)

Three Cup Chicken (San Bei Ji)

三杯雞

Makes 4 to 6 servings

The eponymous "cups" in this recipe's name denote equal parts soy sauce, sesame oil, and rice vinegar. It's a potent, salty, and savory braised chicken dish with these ingredients alone, but the dish really gets its signature flavor from the sheer volume of garlic cloves, thick pieces of ginger, and fresh basil leaves. This recipe's name might underscore the fact that most recipes were passed orally in Taiwan, rather than written, until recent generations. After one taste of it prepared elsewhere, it is quite irresistible to try recreating at home. This dish bears similarities with Hakka-style preparations and red-braised styles of cooking, but its use of basil is refreshingly distinct. It has been enjoyed in Taiwan as a quintessential Taiwanese dish for quite some time.

¾ cup sesame oil

1 (3-inch) piece fresh ginger, peeled and sliced into 12 to 15 thick discs

12 to 15 whole cloves garlic

4 whole scallions, trimmed and cut into 1-inch pieces

2 to 3 small, fresh red chilies, halved or sliced

2 pounds bone-in chicken legs, thighs and wings, cut into roughly 2-inch pieces

1 cup rice wine

1 cup light soy sauce

2 tablespoons sugar

2 cups packed fresh Thai basil leaves

Heat the oil in a large skillet or wok over medium-high heat. Add the ginger, garlic, scallions, and chilies, and cook until just fragrant, about 1 minute. Add the chicken pieces and lightly brown, stirring occasionally, 2 to 3 minutes. Add the rice wine and soy sauce and bring to a boil. Reduce the heat to a simmer and cook, uncovered, until the chicken pieces are cooked through and the sauce has slightly reduced, about 15 minutes. Stir in the sugar until just dissolved. Remove from the heat and stir in the basil. Serve immediately.

Fried Chicken Steaks (Zha Ji Pai)

炸雞排

Makes 4 servings

Like the salty, bite-sized pieces of fried chicken on page 86, a well-seasoned boneless cutlet of fried chicken really needs little accoutrement to be a tasty snack or main course. It's often served in Taiwan with just a dusting of salt and pepper, alone in a bag or atop a mound of fried rice with a side of pickles, sautéed greens, and half a stewed egg as a complete meal.

2 boneless, skinless chicken breasts (about 1 pound total)

1 tablespoon light soy sauce

1 teaspoon sesame oil

1 teaspoon cornstarch

1 teaspoon sugar

¼ teaspoon salt, plus more to taste

¼ teaspoon ground white pepper, plus more to taste

3 to 4 cups vegetable or peanut oil, or more as needed, for frying

4 large eggs, lightly beaten

½ cup water

1 cup sweet potato starch

Slice the chicken breasts into halves to create 4 thin cutlets about ½ inch thick. In a large bowl, mix the soy sauce, sesame oil, cornstarch, sugar, salt, and white pepper. Cover and refrigerate for at least 20 minutes (or up to 1 day).

Add the vegetable oil to a saucepan or wok that is deep enough to completely submerge the chicken cutlets (use more oil if necessary). Heat over medium-high heat until a candy thermometer inserted into the oil (but not touching the pan) reads between 350° to 375°F. Combine the eggs with the water in a bowl and place beside a bowl of the sweet potato starch. Dip each chicken cutlet into the egg wash to coat thoroughly, followed by the starch to coat thoroughly. Shake off any excess starch. Carefully lower a chicken cutlet into the oil. Fry until very golden brown on one side, 2 to 3 minutes, then carefully flip and fry to brown the opposite side, about 2 minutes more. Transfer with tongs to paper towels immediately and repeat with the rest of the chicken.

Sprinkle each piece with salt and white pepper after frying and serve.

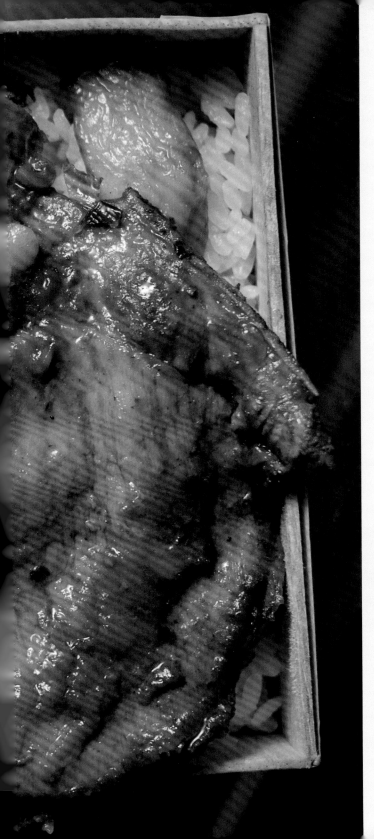

Train Bento in Taiwan

The most pervasive legacy left behind from the Japanese colonial period on Taiwanese food is not actually a food itself—it's the bento box. Boxed meals consisting of several components to be eaten on the go or taken from home have been an everyday commodity in Taiwan ever since.

Taiwanese bento boxes (bian dang in Mandarin, meaning "convenience packs") do not typically feature different compartments, like some Japanese bento. But the food generally follows a similar formula, consisting of a protein, such as a pork chop, piece of chicken, or stewed wheat gluten or tofu; braised cabbage or other greens; a soy sauce–stewed egg; pickles such as pickled radish or mustard greens; and rice. This familiar combo makes for easy grab-and-go meals for businessmen, students, and travelers at train stations or airports. In fact, the classic bento meal of Taiwan was originally sold at train stations only, and still remains ever popular in this setting.

Life in Taiwan changed dramatically with the development and subsequent improvements to its railroad systems. The first railroads were built in the late nineteenth century by the Qing Dynasty. These were later rebuilt and greatly expanded upon by Taiwan's Japanese rulers for the first half of the twentieth century. The Japanese laid the framework for what would eventually grow to become an extensive network of lines, which circled the entire island. These lines connected virtually all walks of Taiwanese life. They also created urban sprawl, leading to the development of outlying suburbs, and reducing street traffic. By the mid-1990s, major cities in Taiwan, including Taichung, Taipei, Tainan, and Kaohsiung, each had high-tech underground subway systems, serving millions of riders per day. Taiwan's high-speed rail, with fast-moving bullet trains modeled after those in Japan, was implemented in 2007. With high-speed rail, one can travel from Taipei to Tainan in less than two hours.

The increasingly efficient mobility throughout the island greatly supported its economic advancements in the latter half of the twentieth century. Businesses could open offices and branches in other cities. Workers could come in and out of cities to earn better wages than where they lived. People who didn't have the means for their own vehicles could now travel easily. Even people who did have cars would often opt for trains out of practicality. Trains in Taiwan are generally smoothly run and very prompt. Stations are well kept, if bustling during peak hours, and usually offer convenience beverages, snacks, and bento meals for sale.

To illustrate what that means with a brief example, I visited a farm in a remote part of Ilan County once. To get there, I got off a train and walked twenty minutes to reach the farm's entrance. I have traveled to numerous farms in Long Island and the Hudson Valley of New York, places that are served by railroad. However, I have never reached a farm there without first passing through long country roads, making a car ride necessary from the closest train station. Much of this is of course due to the compact size and density of the island of Taiwan. The fact remains though that with Taiwan's trains, access to and from cities is possible almost everywhere.

Today's bento box lunches look much the same as those that my parents found in Taiwan decades before. These hot, filling meals never fail to attract customers who line up for them before boarding a train. Home-style and rustic, these meals have persisted as a popular favorite in an ever-advancing society and culture.

A roadside bus stop at night

Shredded Chicken over Rice (Ji Rou Fan)

雞肉飯

Makes 4 to 6 servings

This famous dish hails from Chiayi County, in the southwest of Taiwan. Delicately seasoned shreds of steamed white meat chicken are coated with its own fat and served atop white rice as a hearty comfort food that has now become so popular as to demand stalls for the dish in night markets throughout Taiwan. The original dish utilized shreds of turkey meat instead of chicken; however, turkey is much more rare than chicken, making the true version a delicacy that's often compromised. Try it with either turkey meat or chicken, whichever is more convenient in your area.

2 pounds bone-in, skin-on chicken or turkey pieces (such as breasts or thighs)

½ teaspoon salt

½ teaspoon ground white pepper

1 cup water

1 tablespoon Sichuan peppercorns

2 teaspoons light soy sauce

1 teaspoon sugar

For serving

4 cups steamed rice

2 tablespoons Fried Shallots (see page 52)

¼ cup packed coarsely chopped fresh cilantro

Season the chicken with the salt and white pepper. Prepare a steamer with boiling water underneath. Arrange the chicken on a plate and set inside the steamer. Cover and steam until the chicken pieces are cooked through (the internal temperature close to the bone should reach 180°F), 20 to 25 minutes. Set the chicken and any juices on the plate aside and let cool.

Once cool enough to handle, pull the meat into bite-sized pieces by hand and discard the bones.

Pour the juices from the plate of steamed chicken into a small saucepan along with the water, peppercorns, soy sauce, and sugar. Bring just to a boil, stirring to dissolve the sugar. Reduce the heat to a gentle simmer and cook, uncovered, until the sauce has reduced by about a half, 20 to 30 minutes. Remove from the heat and strain out the peppercorns.

For serving
Divide the rice among 4 to 6 serving bowls and top each with the shredded chicken. Ladle the sauce over each bowl and top with the fried shallots and cilantro to serve.

Wine-Stewed Chicken with Sesame Oil (Ma You Ji)

麻油雞

Makes 6 to 8 servings

It's said in Taiwan that this dish is a must-have for women just after giving birth, to nourish and replenish after expending so much energy. It is a considerable dose of energy, thanks to plenty of rich, bone-in chicken simmered in rice wine and a hefty dose of warming, savory sesame oil. These are really the only ingredients that need be used in the dish, but often, bright red goji berries are sprinkled in toward the end for additional medicinal effect. My friend's grandmother in Taichung once prepared it for me, and she swore by using only wine—never adding any water—as the liquid base for the soup. The resulting broth is very sweet and floral, and little is needed in the way of seasoning with this strong a presence of a classic Taiwanese braising liquid.

1 cup sesame oil

1 (2-inch) piece fresh ginger, peeled and thickly sliced into 8 to 10 discs

2 pounds bone-in, skin-on chicken pieces (such as breasts, thighs, and wings), chopped into bite-sized pieces (preferably at the butcher shop)

2 quarts rice wine

Salt to taste

1 tablespoon dried goji berries

Heat the oil in a large soup pot over medium heat. Add the ginger and cook, stirring occasionally, until sizzling and fragrant, about 10 seconds. Add the chicken pieces and cook, stirring occasionally, until just browned in parts, 2 to 3 minutes. Pour in the rice wine and raise the heat to high. Bring just to a boil and cook for 10 to 15 minutes, skimming off any scum that rises to the top. Reduce the heat to a simmer and cook, uncovered, for about 1 hour. Taste and add salt as desired. Add the goji berries and cook for about 5 minutes longer before serving.

Wine-Stewed Chicken with Sesame Oil (page 177) / Pork Meat Sauce over Rice (page 180)

Pork Meat Sauce over Rice (Lu Rou Fan / Loh Bah Bun)

魯肉飯

Makes 6 to 8 servings

This dish is rustic Taiwanese cuisine at its best. Incredibly rich and flavorful, only a small spoonful of sauce needs to be spread atop a bowl of rice to scoop up every last grain. In the southern counties of Taiwan, this minced meat sauce is usually made with chunkier, hand-chopped pieces of pork belly, rather than the ground pork that's commonly used to prepare the dish nowadays in the north. The sauce can be served atop either rice or noodles for a tasty, if rich, meal. Due to its long-simmered cooking method and use of spare, cheap scraps of meat, it might be thought of as the Taiwanese standard Sunday sauce, or ragu.

2 tablespoons vegetable or peanut oil

2 garlic cloves, minced

2 pounds ground pork or skin-on pork belly, finely chopped or minced

½ cup Fried Shallots (see page 52)

1 tablespoon sugar

1 teaspoon five-spice powder

1 cup rice wine

4 cups water

1 cup light soy sauce

½ cup dark soy sauce

Steamed rice or cooked noodles for 6-8 servings, about 6 cups

Heat the oil in a medium-large saucepan or wok over medium heat. Add the garlic and cook, stirring occasionally, until just sizzling and fragrant, about 1 minute. Add the pork and break up with your spatula into fine pieces as you stir. Cook, stirring frequently, until all the pieces are lightly browned and no longer pinkish in color, 2 to 3 minutes. Stir in the fried shallots, sugar, and five-spice powder and stir until the sugar dissolves, about another minute.

Add the rice wine and bring to a boil. Let boil about 30 seconds, stirring occasionally, then add the water and light and dark soy sauces. Bring to a boil, then reduce to a gentle simmer. Cover and simmer until the sauce is thickened and the meat is very tender, at least 1 hour or preferably 2 hours. Serve with the rice.

Red-Braised Pig's Knuckle (Hong Shao Zhu Jiao)

紅燒豬腳

Makes 4 to 6 small servings

How to make best use of all parts of the animal? Take its toughest, gnarliest pieces and render them into the softest, most blubbery and deliciously infused delicacy you've ever tasted. That's what the Taiwanese have done with the pig's knuckle, a bony piece with little meat to speak of, but much cartilage that renders to sticky bliss with sufficient braising time. Serve with assorted pickled vegetables such as Pickled Mustard Greens Relish (see page 60) or Vinegar-Pickled Cabbage (see page 61).

2 tablespoons vegetable or peanut oil

6 garlic cloves, smashed

6 to 8 thick discs peeled fresh ginger

½ cup packed brown sugar (or rock sugar)

½ cup rice wine

4 cups water

½ cup dark soy sauce

½ cup light soy sauce

2 teaspoons five-spice powder

2 pounds pig knuckles, cut into 2-inch pieces by the butcher

Heat the oil in a large saucepan or wok over medium-high heat. Add the garlic and ginger and cook, stirring, until just sizzling and fragrant, about 30 seconds. Add the sugar and cook, stirring until bubbling, 1 to 2 minutes. Add the rice wine and bring just to a boil, stirring to incorporate the sugar. Add the water, dark and light soy sauces, and five-spice powder and bring to a boil.

Drop in the pig knuckle pieces and return to a boil. Let boil for 10 to 15 minutes, skimming any scum that rises to the top. Reduce the heat to a gentle simmer. Cover and cook until the skin has turned deep red and the pieces are very tender, about 1½ to 2 hours.

Red-Braised Pork Belly (Hong Shao Rou)

紅燒

Makes 4 to 6 small servings

Who needs bacon when pork belly can be cut to sizable chunks and braised, with its fat rendered to gelatinous layers in between tender meat all stained with a savory, soy sauce-based broth? This dish is often found as an addition to a large, multicourse meal, as it's too rich and potently flavored without plenty of contrasting sides. It's sometimes cut to large, square chunks and served with a small pool of braising liquids in a version known as "dong po rou." Here, I've braised the pork belly in a fashion associated most closely with Hunanese homestyle cooking, which my mother often made. Slight variations on spices and preparation techniques can be found throughout Taiwan, but it's a highlight at the table whenever served.

1 pound pork belly

2 tablespoons vegetable or peanut oil

2 whole scallions, trimmed and coarsely chopped

4 garlic cloves, smashed

4 to 6 thick discs peeled fresh ginger

½ cup packed brown sugar

¼ cup rice wine

2 cups water

½ cup light soy sauce

¼ cup dark soy sauce

1 star anise clove

Remove any bones and cut the pork belly into thick pieces about 1½ to 2 inches long.

Heat the oil in a large saucepan or wok over medium-high heat. Arrange the pork belly pieces in a single layer in the pan so that each piece has direct contact with the bottom of the pan. Cook without turning until just lightly browned on one side, about 30 seconds. Flip the pieces over and brown on the opposite sides for just 1 to 2 minutes more. Remove from the pan and set aside.

To the same pan, add the scallions, garlic, and ginger and stir until just sizzling and fragrant, about 30 seconds. Add the sugar and cook, stirring, until bubbling, 1 to 2 minutes. Return the pork pieces to the pan and stir to coat. Add the rice wine and bring just to a boil, stirring to incorporate the sugar. Add the water, light and dark soy sauce, and the star anise and return to a boil. Reduce the heat to a gentle simmer. Cover and cook until the pork is very tender and red-stained, at least 1 hour, preferably 2 hours.

Red-Braised Pork Belly
(page 183)

Hakka-Style Pork Stir-Fry (page 186)

Hakka-Style Pork Stir-Fry (Ke Jia Xiao Chao)

客家小炒

Makes 4 to 6 servings

The Hakka communities of Taiwan are concentrated in the northwest of the island, particularly in Miaoli County, where there are museums and other cultural sightseeing destinations devoted to this heritage. This homely stir-fry is emblematic of its cuisine because it utilizes a tough, less desirable cut of meat and dried seafood, in this case squid (because the Hakka are traditionally mountain people who live far from fresh seafood). While dried squid is easy to find in Taiwan and is traditionally soaked and reconstituted before slicing up in this dish, in the States it is much easier to find fresh squid. So that is what I use here. Also, if Chinese celery (which has much more slender and intensely flavored stalks than the common Western variety) is not to be found, then common celery may be sliced into thin blades for use here instead.

½ pound pork belly

2 tablespoons vegetable or peanut oil

2 garlic cloves, sliced

1 tablespoon peeled and julienned fresh ginger

¼ pound cleaned squid, thinly sliced and tentacles kept intact

1 cup 2-inch pieces Chinese celery or long bias-cut strips common celery

½ cup julienned carrots

1 tablespoon light soy sauce

1 teaspoon chili bean sauce

2 to 3 whole scallions, trimmed and thinly sliced

Bring a small pot of lightly salted water to a boil. Drop in the pork belly and cook until very tender, 20 to 30 minutes. Drain and let cool. Once cool enough to handle, slice thinly into pieces no thicker than ¼ inch.

Heat the oil in a large skillet or wok over medium-high heat. Add the garlic and ginger and cook, stirring occasionally, until sizzling-hot and fragrant, about 10 seconds. Stir in the pork belly and toss briskly for about 1 minute. Stir in the squid, celery, and carrots, and cook, stirring occasionally, until the vegetables are just crisp-tender, 1 to 2 minutes longer. Add the soy sauce and chili bean sauce and stir to coat evenly. Cook until the squid is completely opaque, about 1 minute more. Remove from the heat and stir in the scallions. Serve immediately.

Stir-Fried Slivered Pork with Yellow Chives (Jiu Huang Rou Si)

韭黄肉絲

Makes 4 to 6 servings

These pale slivers of pork are tossed with similarly pale, delicate-tasting Chinese yellow chives. Considered a luxurious ingredient, yellow chives are the same plant as the long, flat-bladed Chinese chives, but they're grown without sunlight soon after sprouting to inhibit the development of chlorophyll and prevent them from turning green. Similar to the beloved white asparagus of Europe, yellow chives are coveted for their milder, sweet flavor and enjoyed with minimal sauces to experience their full taste.

1 pound pork belly, thinly sliced

1 teaspoon cornstarch

1 teaspoon light soy sauce

1 teaspoon sesame oil

¼ teaspoon salt, plus more to taste

¼ teaspoon ground white pepper

2 tablespoons vegetable or peanut oil

1 tablespoon peeled and julienned fresh ginger

1 bunch or about 2 cups packed yellow chives, cut into 2-inch-long pieces

In a large bowl, mix the pork belly with the cornstarch, soy sauce, sesame oil, salt, and white pepper. Cover and refrigerate for at least 20 minutes (or up to 1 day).

Heat the vegetable oil in a skillet or wok over medium-high heat. Add the ginger and cook until sizzling and fragrant, about 10 seconds. Add the pork and cook, stirring frequently, until all the pieces are just slightly browned, 2 to 3 minutes. Add the chives along with a pinch of salt. Cook, stirring briskly, until the chives have softened, 2 to 3 minutes. Taste the dish for seasoning, adding salt if desired, and serve immediately.

Steamed Ground Pork with Pickles (Gua Zai Rou)

瓜仔肉

Makes 4 servings

Who needs sausage when you can season ground pork with spices, including chopped bits of pickles, to steam inside a bowl rather than intestinal casing? This tasty, rich snack or side dish has a distinctively sweet and satisfying flavor and is easy to make at home, on any night of the week. Commonly, the inverted mound of steamed pork is served with a duck egg yolk balanced on top, which once broken into adds even more richness and moisture to every bite. The pickles are a built-in, refreshing touch.

1 pound ground pork

1 cup Sweet Soy-Pickled Cucumbers (see page 62) or store-bought, drained and finely chopped

1 tablespoon pickle brine

1 tablespoon rice wine

1 teaspoon soy sauce

1 teaspoon cornstarch

1 teaspoon sugar

½ teaspoon salt

¼ teaspoon ground white pepper

4 salted duck egg yolks (found in Asian groceries)

Combine the pork, pickles, brine, rice wine, soy sauce, cornstarch, sugar, salt, and white pepper in a bowl and mix lightly by hand. Cover and refrigerate for at least 2 hours (or up to 2 days).

Divide the mixture among 4 rice bowls (or small round ramekins). Prepare a steamer or double boiler with boiling water underneath. Place the bowls inside, cover, and steam until the mixture feels completely firm to the touch and appears opaque, 35 to 40 minutes. Let cool a few minutes.

Gently loosen around the edges of the meat with a spoon. Place a small serving plate on top of the bowl, and flip over to invert. Repeat with the remaining bowls. Carefully place a duck egg yolk on top of each mound of pork and serve.

Stir-Fried Beef with Pickled Mustard Greens and Bean Sprouts (Zha Cai Niu Rou Si)

榨菜牛肉絲

Makes 4 to 6 servings

If fresh vegetables are few, one can always rely on the preserved-food pantry in Taiwan. Not just a condiment or garnish, pickled mustard greens are tossed into this stir-fry to provide pungent flavor, along with crisp bean sprouts. The same dish may be made using thin strips of pork shoulder instead of beef.

1 pound beef flank steak, thinly sliced against the grain

2 teaspoons soy sauce, or more to taste

1 teaspoon cornstarch

½ teaspoon sugar

¼ teaspoon baking soda

¼ teaspoon salt

¼ teaspoon ground white pepper

2 tablespoons vegetable or peanut oil

2 garlic cloves, minced

1 (1-inch) piece fresh ginger, peeled and julienned

2 to 3 small fresh red chilies, thinly sliced on the bias

½ cup shredded Pickled Mustard Greens (see page 57)

2 cups fresh bean sprouts

1 teaspoon sesame oil

In a large bowl, mix the beef with 1 teaspoon of the soy sauce, the cornstarch, sugar, baking soda, salt, and white pepper. Cover and refrigerate for at least 20 minutes (or up to 1 day).

Heat the vegetable oil in a large skillet or wok over medium-high heat. Add the garlic, ginger, and chilies and cook, stirring occasionally, until sizzling and fragrant, about 10 seconds. Add the beef and cook, stirring briskly, until the slices are nearly opaque with no pinkish parts, 2 to 3 minutes. Stir in the pickled mustard greens to mix thoroughly, followed by the bean sprouts. Cook, stirring, until the bean sprouts have turned translucent, 2 to 3 minutes. Add the remaining 1 teaspoon soy sauce, taste for seasoning, adding more soy sauce as desired, and remove from the heat. Stir in the sesame oil and serve immediately.

Sha-Cha Stir-Fried Beef with Watercress
(page 192)

Sha-Cha Stir-Fried Beef with Watercress (Sha Cha Niu Rou Kong Xin Cai)

沙茶牛肉空心菜

Makes 4 to 6 servings

A touch of sha-cha sauce lends savory depth to this otherwise simple stir-fry of beef and green vegetables. Peppery, crisp watercress soaks in its flavors well, and can be substituted with water spinach (a similar vegetable, and Taiwanese favorite), if preferred or in season. This well-balanced stir-fry makes a great meal alone with rice.

1 pound beef flank steak, thinly sliced against the grain

2 teaspoons soy sauce, or more to taste

1 teaspoon cornstarch

¼ teaspoon baking soda

¼ teaspoon salt

¼ teaspoon ground white pepper

2 tablespoons vegetable or peanut oil

2 garlic cloves, minced

1 teaspoon Sha-Cha Sauce (see page 53)

½ lb watercress, chopped into 2-inch-long pieces (about 6 cups)

2 whole scallions, trimmed and thinly sliced

In a bowl, mix the beef with 1 teaspoon of the soy sauce, the cornstarch, baking soda, salt, and white pepper. Cover and refrigerate for at least 20 minutes (or up to 1 day).

Heat the oil in a large skillet or wok over medium heat. Add the garlic and cook, stirring occasionally, until sizzling and fragrant, about 10 seconds. Add the beef and cook, stirring briskly, until the slices are nearly opaque with no pinkish parts, 2 to 3 minutes. Stir in the sha-cha sauce followed by the watercress and stir to distribute evenly. Cook, stirring occasionally, until the watercress has wilted to deep-green leaves while the stalks are still slightly crisp, 3 to 4 minutes. Add the remaining 1 teaspoon soy sauce and taste for seasoning, adding additional soy sauce if desired. Remove from the heat and toss in the scallions. Serve immediately.

Pan-Fried Pork Liver with Sweet and Sour Glaze (Jian Zhu Gan)

煎豬肝

Makes 4 to 6 servings

Offal cuts like liver and intestine are no strangers to everyday Taiwanese cooking. Pork livers are often cut into thick slabs to cook gently and float atop soups, but here they are pan-seared and tossed in a tangy sauce to help mask their distinctive flavor. If you're not generally a fan of liver, you might change your mind after trying this dish.

1 pound pork liver

2 teaspoons cornstarch

1 tablespoon plus 1 teaspoon sugar

1 teaspoon sesame oil

¼ teaspoon salt

¼ teaspoon ground white pepper

¼ cup vegetable or peanut oil

½ cup rice wine

¼ cup light soy sauce

1 teaspoon rice vinegar

¼ cup cold water

2 tablespoons coarsely chopped fresh cilantro, for garnish

Rinse the pork liver under cold water for 5 minutes, or until no more blood is released when pressed. Pat dry thoroughly with paper towels. Slice lengthwise into ovals about ¼ inch thick. In a bowl, mix the liver pieces with 1 teaspoon of the cornstarch, 1 teaspoon of the sugar, the sesame oil, salt, and white pepper. Cover and refrigerate for at least 10 minutes (or up to 2 hours).

Heat about half the vegetable oil in a large skillet or wok over high heat. Once the oil is very hot and beginning to pop and sizzle a little, arrange as many pork liver pieces as will fit in a single layer in the pan so that the bottoms have full contact with the pan (you will need to work in batches). Sear for about 15 seconds without stirring. Peek underneath the pieces, and if gently browned, flip and sear the opposite sides until just browned, about 15 seconds more. Remove from the pan and set aside. Repeat with the remaining vegetable oil and livers.

To the same pan used for searing the livers, add the rice wine and bring to a boil, scraping the pan to release any browned bits. Add the soy sauce, vinegar, and the remaining 1 tablespoon sugar and stir to dissolve the sugar. In a separate bowl, stir together the remaining 1 teaspoon cornstarch and the water. Once the sauce is boiling, stir in the cornstarch mixture and continue to cook, stirring, until the sauce is thickened, about 30 seconds. Return the livers to the pan and gently toss to coat them thoroughly. Transfer to a serving dish and garnish with the cilantro. Serve immediately.

Fried Rice with Pork and Tea Leaves (Cha Ye Chao Fan)

茶葉炒飯

Makes 4 to 6 servings

The inventive use of toasted tea leaves lends this otherwise ordinary fried rice a smoky depth. In the high mountains of Taiwan where tea is grown, local shops and restaurants often specialize in tea-inflected dishes, or tea cuisine (see page 239). Most Taiwanese tea leaves are black oolong varieties that range in nuance and subtlety. Look for fresh packs of whole, dried black tea leaves of this variety, as preground or very old tea won't have as much flavor.

½ pound pork shoulder, thinly sliced

1 teaspoon light soy sauce

1 teaspoon sesame oil

½ teaspoon cornstarch

¼ teaspoon salt, plus more to taste

¼ teaspoon ground white pepper, plus more to taste

2 tablespoons whole black tea leaves

¼ cup vegetable or peanut oil

4 large eggs, beaten

½ cup finely diced carrots

1 cup fresh or thawed frozen green peas

4 cups cooked white rice (preferably day-old rice)

3 whole scallions, trimmed and thinly sliced

In a large bowl, marinate the pork in the soy sauce, sesame oil, cornstarch, salt, and white pepper. Cover and refrigerate for at least 20 minutes (or up to 1 day).

Heat a dry skillet or wok over medium-low heat and add the tea leaves. Cook, swirling or shaking the pan occasionally, until the tea leaves are very fragrant and lightly toasted, 2 to 3 minutes (remove from the heat immediately if you detect a burning smell). Remove the leaves from the pan and set aside to cool for a few minutes. Crush the leaves gently with a mortar and pestle.

Heat 1 tablespoon of the vegetable oil in a large skillet or wok over medium-high heat. Once the oil is very hot and beginning to pop and sizzle a little, add the pork and stir briskly. Cook, stirring frequently, until the pieces are lightly browned and no longer pinkish in color, 1 to 2 minutes. Remove the pork from the pan and set aside.

Season the beaten eggs with a pinch each of salt and white pepper. Heat another tablespoon of oil in the wok and once very hot, pour in the eggs. Cook, stirring to scramble and break up the eggs into small chunks, until just fully cooked, about 1 minute. Transfer the eggs to a dish and set aside. Heat another tablespoon of oil in the same pan and once hot, add the carrots and peas. Reduce the heat to low and cook, stirring occasionally, until the carrots are just softened and the peas are bright green in color, 2 to 3 minutes. Transfer to a dish.

Heat the remaining 1 tablespoon oil in the same pan and, once hot, add the rice. Stir immediately to break up any chunks, and season liberally with pinches of salt and white pepper. Stir in the crushed tea leaves and cook, stirring, until incorporated throughout the rice. Return the pork, scrambled eggs, peas, and carrots to the pan and toss to combine thoroughly. Turn off the heat and stir in the scallions. Taste for seasoning, adding salt and pepper as desired, and serve.

Shredded Pork and Napa Cabbage Stew (Xi Lu Rou)

西滷肉

Makes 6 to 8 servings

This home-style dish can be found in Taiwan's Ilan County, a largely rural and poor region comparatively. However, Ilan households tend to be very welcoming and hospitable. There is a tradition in Taiwan of street banquets, where visitors may sample the home cooking of households who serve them up along the street. Cooks receive enormous pride when their dish is well liked at these casual street fairs, also known as "water flowing banquets." This is one such dish that may be commonly found served at them— simple to make yet hearty and satisfying.

½ pound pork shoulder, thinly sliced

1 teaspoon soy sauce

½ teaspoon cornstarch

½ teaspoon sugar

¼ teaspoon salt, plus more to taste

¼ teaspoon ground white pepper, plus more to taste

3 tablespoons vegetable or peanut oil

4 to 6 dried shiitake mushrooms, soaked in 2 cups cold water until fully reconstituted (about 30 minutes), de-stemmed and thinly sliced

½ cup julienned carrots

½ cup julienned fresh bamboo shoots (see Note, page 159) or canned, rinsed well

1 pound napa cabbage, shredded

6 cups water or Basic Pork Soup Stock (see page 128)

1 teaspoon sesame oil

2 whole scallions, trimmed and thinly sliced

1 cup packed coarsely chopped fresh cilantro sprigs

2 tablespoons Fried Shallots (see page 52)

In a large bowl, marinate the pork in the soy sauce, cornstarch, sugar, salt, and white pepper. Cover and refrigerate for at least 20 minutes (or up to 1 day).

Heat 1 tablespoon of the vegetable oil in a large pot over medium-high heat until it begins to pop and sizzle, about 30 seconds. Add the pork. Cook, stirring briskly, until the pieces are lightly browned and no longer pinkish, 1 to 2 minutes. Remove the pork from the pan and set aside. Heat another tablespoon of the oil and once just hot, add the mushrooms, carrots, and bamboo shoots along with a pinch of salt. Cook, stirring frequently, for another 1 to 2 minutes. Remove from the pan.

Add the remaining 1 tablespoon oil to the same pan and once hot, stir in the cabbage and a couple pinches of salt. Cook, stirring occasionally, until the cabbage has wilted slightly, 2 to 3 minutes. Add the water and bring just to a boil. Return the pork, mushrooms, carrots, and bamboo shoots to the pot and stir to combine. Return just to a boil, then reduce the heat to a simmer. Cook, uncovered, for at least 30 minutes, preferably 1 hour. Taste for seasoning, adding salt and pepper as desired. Finally, drizzle in the sesame oil. Serve garnished with the scallions, cilantro, and fried shallots.

Seafood

Pan-Fried Whole Fish with Garlic, Ginger, and Scallions (page 206)

Fried Fishcakes (Tian Bu La)

甜不辣

Makes about 4 servings

This dish's name is a phonetic translation of "tempura," and originated with the Japanese penchant for frying small, snacklike morsels until crisp and bubbly. Once fried, these morsels are sometimes then soaked in a soup, so that their light, spongy texture absorbs the broth. However, they can also be served crispy and topped with a sweet-and-sour sauce like Sweet-and-Sour Tomato–Based Sauce (page 54) or Sweet-and-Sour Citrus and Soy–Based Sauce (page 55).

¾ pound skinless white-fleshed fish fillets (such as cod), cut into 1-inch chunks

¼ cup cornstarch

1 teaspoon sugar

1 teaspoon rice wine

1 teaspoon salt

¼ teaspoon ground white pepper

½ cup ice-cold water

3 to 4 cups vegetable or peanut oil, or more as needed, for frying

Sweet-and-Sour Tomato–Based Sauce (see page 54) or Sweet-and-Sour Citrus and Soy–Based Sauce (see page 55)

In a large bowl, combine the fish with the cornstarch, sugar, rice wine, salt, and white pepper and mix to coat the fish thoroughly. Transfer to a food processor or blender and pulse several times, stopping to scrape down the sides, until the mixture becomes a smooth paste, about 2 minutes. While pulsing, slowly pour in the water. Continue to process until the mixture is a very smooth puree with no visible chunks. Transfer to a bowl, cover, and refrigerate at least 2 hours or up to overnight.

Add the oil to a saucepan or wok so that the oil is deep enough to completely submerge a tablespoon-sized drop of fishcake batter (add more oil if necessary). Heat over medium-high heat until a candy thermometer inserted into the oil (but not touching the pan) reads between 350° and 375°F. When cooking, adjust the heat if necessary to retain this temperature.

The cakes can be made in any shape, but long, squiggly or flattened oval-like pieces are common. Just be sure the cakes are roughly the same size, so that they will cook in the same amount of time. Scoop the fishcake batter with a spoon, then push the batter to the edge of the spoon to drop it into the oil in irregular-shaped tubes. Repeat with more batter, working in batches of 4 to 6 cakes at a time so that they fry without touching one another. Fry, turning occasionally, until just lightly golden-brown all around, 3 to 4 minutes. Transfer immediately to paper towels. Repeat with the rest of the batter. Serve immediately with your preferred sauce.

"Q" Texture

The ideal of the fish ball or meatball in Taiwan is very different from that of Western equivalents. This is mostly concerning its texture. Rather than loosely formed, chunky-textured crab cakes, fish cakes, or Italian meatballs found in the States, the most common types of fish balls and meatballs in Taiwan feature a smooth, pureed mixture of proteins and starches shaped into a tight ball that's springy and somewhat bouncy.

Assorted fish cakes in a market

Springy and bouncy: these are perhaps the best approximations of the meaning of the word described in Taiwan only by the roman letter "Q." To say that a food is "Q" is certainly a compliment. To gush as an eater, "How Q!" would imply that the dish had attained an excellent state of texture, not dull or too soft. This sometimes runs counter to fixed Western ideas; other words that could be used to describe "Q" are not complimentary among connoisseurs: chewy, gummy, and rubbery.

Taiwanese eaters are almost as concerned with texture as they are with taste. Hence, we find examples of rather tasteless elements in dishes that only add to textural appeal: the clear jellylike starch in oyster omelets, the skin of ba-wan or meatball mochi, and the tapioca pearls found in teas. Understanding the enjoyment of chewing on these bouncy things—coated with tasty flavors—is key to appreciating these dishes. It's also key to enjoying meatballs and fish balls, which are commonly added to soups and noodle dishes in Taiwan. In many restaurants, one can often order the addition of one or two of these morsels to any bowl they choose. In households, frozen packages of meatballs and fish balls are dropped into broths for convenient, easy kids' meals (which I enjoyed in my youth). However, it is rare for one to make such foods from scratch at home. Much like hot dogs and sausages, these processed meats are complicated to produce in a home kitchen, but widely available in grocery stores. In Taiwan, one can even buy packs of frozen fish paste, which is used to form into balls, nuggets, or slivers such as those found in Rou Geng (page 130). The recipe for making basic fish paste is quite the same as the recipe in this chapter for Fried Fishcakes (Tian Bu La; see page 201). Instead of deep-frying the pieces, one can form the paste into any shape they wish and drop it into boiling water. Because these gummy, chewy bites are so well liked by children, there is a plethora of fish balls and fish cakes commercially available in various different colors,

shapes, and sizes (like Hello Kitty, for instance). The light flavor of white fish—and often squid or cuttlefish—mellowed by considerable amounts of starch is mild on the palate. Many cakes feature a combination of meat-based and fish-based pastes, providing an attractive contrast of taste and color. They're not solely for kids, either. On my latest visit home, my mother pulled a new fish ball out of the freezer that had a chunky, lu rou–style pork sauce stuffed inside. Once heated through, these fish balls exploded like a ravioli when bitten into.

It might seem a little counterintuitive to grind up fresh, boneless fish fillets in order to make fish paste for fried fish cakes, as I felt it was while I was recipe testing. Traditionally, fish balls and cakes are made from scraps of seafood too small to use for serving, such as those bits of meat scraped from the fish bones when filleting. Fish cakes are therefore a practical use for this byproduct of commercial seafood processing. For an island that eats as much seafood as Taiwan, it is no wonder that these bound, bouncy fish cakes are so commonly eaten. Not too long ago it was more commonplace to find homemade versions, but today they're an industrial product, made in large quantities in factories. Furthermore, achieving the perfect level of "Q" is not intuitive for the average home cook.

However, given the rise in awareness about food additives in Taiwan, where many consumers are concerned about the safety of their food and prefer natural, non-GMO, and less chemical-addled products, I thought it would be fun to backtrack to a very simple, additive-free formula for fish paste. With just fresh fish, starch, and a little seasoning, a clean-tasting fish paste can indeed be made for many versatile purposes.

Squid fishing boats at harbor

Pan-Fried Whole Fish with Garlic, Ginger, and Scallions (Cong Jiang Quan Yu)

蔥薑全魚

Makes 4 to 6 servings

This is Taiwan's style of pan-frying a fish: with copious fresh herbs, and plenty of sauce. Salty, pungent, and slightly sweet, the sauce is made just after pan-frying the fish in the same pan, to drizzle liberally on top. It's a one-pot dish fit for the finest banquet tables, but also commonly served up at seafood market vendor stands.

1 (1½- to 2-pound) whole white-fleshed fish (such as black bass)

¼ teaspoon salt

¼ teaspoon ground white pepper

¼ cup vegetable or peanut oil

1 (2-inch) piece fresh ginger, peeled and julienned

4 garlic cloves, thinly sliced

1 cup rice wine

1 tablespoon sugar

¼ cup light soy sauce

4 whole scallions, trimmed and thinly sliced

Rinse the fish and pat dry with paper towels. Lightly score the fish with 2 slashes on each side (not deep enough to hit the bone). Rub the salt and white pepper across its surface and inside its cavity.

Heat the oil in a large skillet or wok big enough to fit the whole fish over medium-high heat. Once the oil is very hot and beginning to pop and sizzle a little, carefully place the fish on one side in the oil. Cook undisturbed until gently browned on the bottom, 2 to 3 minutes. Carefully flip the fish over (with the help of two spatulas if necessary). Brown the opposite side of the fish for another 2 to 3 minutes. Touch the top of the fish to check if it feels firm, and peek inside the slash to ensure that the flesh appears to be entirely opaque and not clear white toward the center. Once fully cooked, transfer the fish carefully to a serving platter.

To the same pan, add the ginger and garlic and stir until fragrant, about 10 seconds. Add the rice wine and bring to a boil. Stir in the sugar and soy sauce until the sugar is thoroughly dissolved. Stir in half of the scallions and remove from the heat. Pour the sauce over the plated fish. Garnish with the remaining scallions and serve immediately.

Steamed Cod with Five-Flavor Sauce (Wu Wei Yu)

五味魚

Makes 4 to 6 servings

This unique sauce features visible chunks of minced fresh cilantro, scallions, ginger, chilies, and garlic enveloped in a slightly sweet ketchup base, to comprise its "five flavors." It's often served with simply prepared seafood, such as squid, oysters, or abalone. Here, it's drizzled generously on fluffy, steamed chunks of boneless cod fillet. Feel free to substitute another mild-tasting, white-fleshed fish that's fresh or in season near you instead.

For the fish

1 pound cod fillets, trimmed of any pin bones with tweezers

1 tablespoon rice wine

1 teaspoon cornstarch

¼ teaspoon salt

¼ teaspoon ground white pepper

For the sauce

½ cup ketchup

1 teaspoon light soy sauce

1 teaspoon sugar

1 teaspoon cornstarch

¼ cup cold water

1 tablespoon peeled and minced fresh ginger

2 small fresh red chilies, finely chopped

1 tablespoon minced garlic

1 tablespoon packed finely chopped fresh cilantro

1 tablespoon packed finely chopped fresh scallions

For the fish

Rinse the fish and pat dry with paper towels. Rub the fillets with the rice wine, cornstarch, salt, and white pepper. Cover and refrigerate for at least 10 minutes (or up to 2 hours).

For the sauce

Combine the ketchup, soy sauce, and sugar in a small saucepan and bring just to a boil. In a separate bowl, stir together the cornstarch and water. Stir the cornstarch mixture into the ketchup mixture. Cook, stirring, until the mixture bubbles and thickens a little, about 10 seconds. Remove from the heat and let cool completely. Once cool, stir in the ginger, chilies, garlic, cilantro, and scallions. (You can do this up to 2 days ahead and store, covered, in the refrigerator.)

Prepare a steamer or double boiler with boiling water underneath. Place the fish on a plate and cover inside the steamer. Steam for 4 to 5 minutes, then peek inside. The fish pieces should feel firm to the touch and be opaque rather than clear white in any areas. Remove the fish from the steamer and let cool a few moments. Arrange the fish on a platter and drizzle liberally with the sauce. Serve immediately.

Pan-Fried Fish with Peanuts and Cilantro (Xiang Jian Yu Pai)

香煎魚排

Makes 4 to 6 servings

Larger fish are often sliced to meaty, steaklike midsections with the bone and skin intact in Taiwan. These pieces are much easier to sear and flip in a pan than a boneless fillet, and are great for doling out small portions at a family-style table. You can use any type of fish for this preparation, but oilier species like salmon or swordfish are preferable. These will provide much flavor and juiciness on their own, accented minimally with classic Taiwanese garnishes of cilantro and crushed peanut powder.

1 pound fish steaks or ½- to 1-inch thick midsection slices (ask your fishmonger to slice them)

½ teaspoon salt

¼ teaspoon ground white pepper

¼ cup vegetable or peanut oil

½ cup Crushed Peanut Powder (see page 63)

2 cups coarsely chopped fresh cilantro

Rinse the fish and pat dry with paper towels. Season all over with the salt and white pepper. Heat the oil in a large skillet or wok over medium-high heat. Once the oil is very hot and beginning to sizzle or pop, arrange as many fish steaks as will fit in a single layer in the pan so that the undersides have full contact with the bottom of the pan (you will probably need to work in batches of 2 at a time). Sear for about 1 minute, then peek underneath; if the fish is lightly browned, carefully flip it over. Sear the opposite side until lightly browned and the fish feels firm and cooked through to the touch, another 1 to 2 minutes. Transfer to a serving dish. Repeat with the remaining batches of fish steaks.

Arrange the fish steaks on a platter and shower generously with the peanut powder and the cilantro. Serve immediately.

Three Cup Squid (San Bei Xiao Juan)

三杯小卷

Makes 4 to 6 servings

The beloved flavor profile of Three Cup Chicken (see page 169) is borrowed here to make a tasty squid dish. However, this dish is much quicker to cook than the braised pieces of bone-in chicken. Be sure to have all your ingredients prepped and ready to toss into the pan nearby, as squid only takes a few moments to cook through, and if cooked too long it will become tough and chewy.

½ cup sesame oil

1 (1-inch) piece fresh ginger, peeled and julienned

4 garlic cloves, finely chopped

2 small fresh red chilies, finely chopped

1 pound cleaned squid, sliced into rings and tentacles kept intact

½ cup rice wine

½ cup light soy sauce

2 teaspoons sugar

1 cup packed fresh Thai basil leaves

Heat the oil in a large skillet or wok over medium-high heat. Add the ginger, garlic, and chilies. Cook, stirring, until the oil is very hot and the herbs are very fragrant and sizzling, about 10 seconds. Add the squid and cook, stirring briskly, for about 30 seconds. Pour in the rice wine, soy sauce, and sugar and stir until bubbling and the sugar has dissolved. Remove from the heat and stir in the basil. Serve immediately.

Oysters with Black Bean Sauce (Yin Chi E Zai / Yin Xi O Ah)

蔭豉蚵仔

Makes 4 to 6 servings

A simple way to prepare one of Taiwan's most prolific types of seafood, this dish is a favorite among home cooks. The briny taste of oysters is complemented by fermented black beans studded throughout, for little pops of flavor along with the plump oysters. This dish is also wonderfully quick to cook, so have all your ingredients prepped and ready to toss into the pan.

1 teaspoon cornstarch

¼ cup cold water

2 tablespoons vegetable or peanut oil

2 garlic cloves, minced

1 leek or 2 large leeks, white and light green parts only, trimmed and finely chopped

2 dozen oysters, preshucked or shucked at home

1 tablespoon fermented black beans

Salt and ground white pepper to taste

In a small bowl, stir together the cornstarch and water and set near the stove.

Heat the oil in a skillet or wok over medium-high heat and add the garlic. Cook, stirring, until fragrant, about 10 seconds. Add the leek and cook for another minute, stirring occasionally. Add the oysters and black beans and stir to distribute evenly. Cook until the oysters appear firmer, 1 to 2 minutes. Give the cornstarch mixture a final stir to loosen it up and pour it into the pan. Stir and allow the mixture to bubble and thicken. Add salt and white pepper to taste, and serve immediately.

Fried Oysters
(E Zai Su / O Ah So)
蚵仔酥
Makes 4 to 6 small servings

At seafood shacks in just about every part of the world, one can find crispy, fried fresh seafood. Taiwan is no exception, and its plentiful oysters make this catch a popular choice for deep-frying in a crispy, golden batter. As with the Fried Chicken Bites (see page 86), Taiwanese cooks love to sprinkle it with fried leaves of basil as a signature flourish.

4 large eggs, beaten

¼ cup water

¼ teaspoon salt, plus more to taste

¼ teaspoon white pepper, plus more to taste

1 cup sweet potato starch

2 dozen oysters, preshucked or shucked at home

4 to 6 cups vegetable or peanut oil, or more as needed, for frying

1 bunch fresh Thai basil leaves

Combine the eggs, water, salt, and white pepper in a large bowl. Place a bowl of the sweet potato starch beside it. Submerge the oysters in the egg mixture. Lift out one at a time and roll in the sweet potato starch to coat thoroughly. Shake off any excess and set aside. Repeat with the rest of the oysters.

Meanwhile, add the oil to a pot so that it is at least 4 inches deep (use more oil if necessary). Heat over medium-high heat until a candy thermometer inserted into the oil (but not touching the pan) reads between 325° and 350°F. Drop in 4 to 6 oysters at a time, or as many as will fit without touching one another in the oil. Cook, turning occasionally with tongs, until the oysters develop a crispy, golden crust all around, about 2 minutes. Remove the finished oysters with a slotted spoon and transfer immediately to paper towels. Repeat with the rest of the oysters. Finally, toss the basil leaves in the hot oil and fry until translucent, about 10 seconds. Remove carefully and transfer to paper towels to cool. Sprinkle the oysters all over with salt and white pepper and serve with the fried basil leaves.

Chilled Oysters with Black Vinegar, Cilantro, and Shallots (Cong Xiang Xian E / Cong Xiang Xian Ke)

蔥香鮮蚵

Makes 4 to 6 servings

For as much as Taiwan eats oysters, you won't find much in the way of raw oysters on the island. Cooked, then chilled oysters are much more aligned with Taiwanese preferences, and when combined with tangy vinegar and fresh herbs, the result is similar to enjoying them on the half-shell with mignonette. I greatly enjoyed the fresh taste of this easy dish at a home dinner in Taiwan, and gave it a couple tweaks of my own with the addition of fried shallots and lots of black vinegar to complement the oysters' natural brininess.

2 dozen oysters, preshucked or shucked at home

¼ cup black vinegar

Salt and ground white pepper to taste

1 bunch fresh cilantro, leaves and stems coarsely chopped

½ cup Fried Shallots (see page 52)

Bring a large pot of water to a boil. Prepare an ice water bath in a large bowl and set aside. Drop the oysters into the boiling water and cook until they all float to the surface, 3 to 5 minutes. Remove with a slotted spoon and transfer the oysters immediately to the ice water bath to cool. After a few seconds, drain and transfer the oysters to a serving dish.

Sprinkle the vinegar evenly over the oysters and then sprinkle with salt and white pepper. Scatter the cilantro on top, followed by the fried shallots. Serve immediately.

Basil Clams
(Ta Xiang Ge Li)
塔香蛤蜊
Makes 4 to 6 servings

The tiny, tender manila clam is the most popular type for cooking in Taiwan. These are delicate tasting and quick to cook, and they're actually the same species of clam as littlenecks, only harvested at a younger stage. Seek them out in Asian seafood markets or any fresh seafood market with a wide selection. This simple braise infuses them with lots of classic, pungent Taiwanese flavor.

2 tablespoons vegetable or peanut oil

1 (1-inch) piece fresh ginger, peeled and julienned

4 garlic cloves, finely chopped

3 to 4 small fresh red chilies, finely chopped

2 cups rice wine

1 tablespoon light soy sauce

2 pounds manila clams, rinsed and scrubbed

1 cup packed fresh Thai basil leaves

Heat the oil in a large pot with a lid over medium-high heat. Once hot, add the ginger, garlic, and chilies and cook, stirring, until fragrant, about 30 seconds. Add the rice wine and soy sauce and bring to a boil. Drop in the clams and cover the pot. Let cook for 3 to 4 minutes, then peek inside. If all the clams are opened, remove from the heat; if not, cover and cook until all the clams have opened, another 1 to 2 minutes. Discard any clams that do not open after about 6 minutes. Stir in the basil and transfer the clams to a deep dish or bowl and serve immediately.

Wine-Marinated Clams (Yan Ge Li / Xin Ha Ma)

醃蛤蜊

Makes 4 to 6 servings

This dish could be referred to as "drunken clams," for the clams are soaked in rice wine overnight to absorb all the flavor and served simply (much like the Shanghai specialty, drunken chicken). The wine fully seeps into the clams over the course of several hours, so that the wine's acidity slowly cooks them in a manner that's similar to making ceviche. It's an unconventional way to prepare clams, but if you love the sweet flavor of rice wine, then this is an unconventionally good, fresh-tasting seafood dish.

2 pounds manila clams, rinsed and scrubbed

4 cups rice wine, or more as needed

4 garlic cloves, finely chopped

2 to 3 small fresh red chilies, finely chopped

¼ cup light soy sauce

Combine the clams, wine, garlic, and chilies in a large bowl or dish so that most of the clams are fully submerged in the wine (add more wine if necessary). Cover with a wet paper towel and refrigerate for at least 6 hours, or up to 12 hours. Most of the clams should be peeking open; discard any that have not opened. Drain the wine from the clams and drizzle all over with the soy sauce. Serve immediately.

Clams Braised with Loofah Squash (Ge Li Si Gua)

蛤蜊絲瓜

Makes 4 to 6 servings

One well-liked way of preparing clams in Taiwan is in a light, clear braise alongside chunks of loofah squash (or gourd). The latter is a mild-tasting summer squash that cooks to soft, slightly viscous and spongy pieces when braised. If you find loofah squash in an Asian market (sometimes called Chinese okra), be sure to peel its tough outer skin thoroughly before slicing. I find that green zucchini or yellow summer squash is an apt substitute, and commonly found in the States.

2 medium zucchini or summer squash or 1 loofah gourd, peeled

2 tablespoons vegetable or peanut oil

2 garlic cloves, minced

Salt and ground white pepper to taste

1 cup Basic Pork Soup Stock (see page 128) or water

2 pounds manila clams, rinsed and scrubbed

1 teaspoon cornstarch

¼ cup cold water

Trim the ends from the squash or gourd. Cut in half lengthwise and then into half-rounds about ½ inch thick.

Heat the oil in a large skillet or saucepan with a lid over medium heat. Add the garlic and cook for about 10 seconds, followed by the squash. Season with a pinch each of salt and white pepper and cook, stirring occasionally, until the squash softens slightly and is coated with the seasonings, about 1 minute. Add the stock and bring to a boil. Drop in the clams and cover the skillet. Let cook, covered, for 3 to 4 minutes. Peek inside; if all the clams have opened, remove the lid. If not, cover and continue to cook until all the clams have opened, another 1 to 2 minutes. Discard any clams that have not opened after about 6 minutes of cooking.

Stir together the cornstarch and water in a separate bowl. Bring the clam and squash mixture to a boil, then pour in the cornstarch mixture. Cook, stirring, until the mixture thickens, about 10 seconds. Season with salt and white pepper to taste and serve immediately.

Clams Braised with Loofah Squash (page 221) / Pan-Fried Shrimp with Tea Leaves (page 224)

Crab Fried Rice (page 227)

Pan-Fried Shrimp with Tea Leaves (Cha Ye Da Xia)

茶葉大蝦

Makes 4 to 6 servings

Taiwanese eaters do not mind peeling shrimp shells and heads at the table, and feel strongly that sautéing them in their shells retains their sweet flavor and juiciness better than peeling before cooking. This dish could be cooked either way, however, for its main attraction is a unique, herbal garnish of crushed and toasted tea leaves, along with crisped shallots and fresh herbs. This aromatic topping can be showered liberally when the shrimp are cooked in their shells, as much of it won't be ultimately eaten once the shrimp are peeled at the table. If making the dish with peeled shrimp, you may want to decrease the amount of ground tea, fried shallots, and especially chilies.

¼ cup loose black oolong tea leaves

2 tablespoons vegetable or peanut oil

4 garlic cloves, finely chopped

3 to 4 small fresh red chilies, finely chopped

2 pounds whole shrimp with heads and shells on (see note above about substituting peeled shrimp)

Salt and white pepper to taste

2 tablespoons Fried Shallots (see page 52)

½ cup packed coarsely chopped fresh cilantro

Heat a dry skillet or wok over medium-low heat and add the tea leaves. Cook, swirling or shaking the pan occasionally, until the tea leaves are very fragrant and lightly toasted, 2 to 3 minutes (reduce the heat immediately if you detect a burning smell). Remove from the pan and set aside. Cool for a few more minutes and then crush the leaves gently with a mortar and pestle.

Heat the oil in a large skillet or wok over medium-high heat. Once hot, add the garlic and chilies and cook until fragrant, about 10 seconds. Add the shrimp and stir. Cook, stirring frequently, until the shrimp have all turned bright orange in color, about 2 minutes. Season to taste with salt and white pepper and sprinkle in half the crushed tea leaves and half the fried shallots. Give a final toss and transfer to a serving dish. Sprinkle the remaining tea leaves, fried shallots, and the cilantro across the top and serve immediately.

Deep-Fried Shrimp Rolls (Xia Juan)

蝦卷

Makes 8 rolls

This street food snack hails from the old district of Anping in the city of Tainan. Anping was home to one of the first settlements of the Dutch in Taiwan, and today, visitors can visit the Dutch-built Fort Zeelandia (or Anping Castle) as a tourist attraction. There are no remaining sixteenth-century houses to speak of otherwise in Anping, but its narrow, winding streets have a different atmosphere from the rest of the city. This old neighborhood also boasts a robust food vendor tradition, and because it's right on the water, seafood-based snacks and dishes are bountiful. The signature way to make these shrimp-based rolls in Taiwan would be to wrap them in caul fat, a spotty, lacelike membrane of pork fat. This gives the resulting roll an extra savory flavor and aroma. However, one may substitute basic spring roll wrappers—if not to quite the same effect—as I've done in this recipe, which still provides for a thin, crispy, golden crust.

1 pound shrimp, peeled, deveined, and coarsely chopped

1 cup fishcake batter for Fried Fishcakes (see page 201)

2 large eggs, lightly beaten

¼ cup water chestnuts, finely chopped

¼ cup finely chopped celery (preferably Chinese celery)

¼ cup finely chopped whole scallions

¼ teaspoon salt

¼ teaspoon ground white pepper

8 fresh (4- to 6-inch) round spring roll wrappers

4 cups vegetable or peanut oil, or more as needed, for frying

In a large bowl, combine the shrimp, fishcake batter, eggs, water chestnuts, celery, scallions, salt, and white pepper. Mix well by hand to incorporate thoroughly.

To assemble each roll, spread a spring roll wrapper on a flat surface. Spread about ¼ cup of the filling mixture along the bottom edge of the wrapper, leaving at least ½ inch at the sides (be sure not to stuff the rolls too full, or the ingredients inside will not cook through). Fold the sides over the filling and then roll from the bottom up until the filling is fully enclosed in the wrapper. Moisten along the inside of the top edge with water before sealing it shut. Repeat with the remaining spring roll wrappers and filling.

Add the oil to a wok or pot so that it is deep enough to submerge the rolls (use more oil if necessary). Heat over medium-high heat until a candy thermometer inserted into the oil (but not touching the pan) reads between 350° and 375°F. When cooking, adjust the heat if necessary to maintain this temperature. Carefully drop in the spring rolls, working in batches if necessary, so that the rolls fry without sticking together. Let fry for about 2 minutes, then turn the rolls over with chopsticks or tongs. Continue frying until the wrappers are deeply golden in color, another 2 to 3 minutes. Transfer immediately to paper towels. Serve immediately.

Wine-Braised Shrimp (Shao Jiu Xia)

燒酒蝦

Makes 4 to 6 servings

Shrimp are thought to be sweetest when cooked in the shell by the Taiwanese. Here, the natural sweetness of the shellfish is amplified with rice wine as a braising liquid. The resulting broth turns a rich orange color, and is delicious to spoon onto white rice.

2 tablespoons vegetable or peanut oil

2 garlic cloves, minced

2 pounds whole shrimp, with heads and shells on

2 cups rice wine

Salt and ground white pepper to taste

Heat the oil in a large skillet or wok over medium-high heat. Add the garlic and cook, stirring, until very fragrant and hot, about ten seconds. Add the shrimp and cook, stirring briskly, to bring out the fragrance of the shells, about 30 seconds. Pour in the rice wine and bring to a boil. Let boil until all the shrimp are thoroughly orange and opaque, 2 to 3 minutes. Season the broth with salt and white pepper to taste and serve immediately.

Crab Fried Rice (Xie Rou Chao Fan)

蟹肉炒飯

Makes 4 to 6 servings

When crabs are in season in Taiwan in the fall, madness ensues. People flock to coastal cities for a day trip of eating as much crab as they can. There are crab festivals and street fairs occur, and restaurants serve crab in myriad ways. These crustaceans come in many species off the Taiwanese coast; the more impressively sized, of course, the easier for cracking open and enjoying more of its meat. I suggest using Dungeness crab for this fried rice dish. You could substitute live crab with fresh lump crabmeat from a reputable source, but then you wouldn't have the shells, which are a classic decorative touch. Also, the Taiwanese like to eat the roe from the insides of the crab shells, and this is kept on the half shell to enjoy.

1 large live Dungeness crab (about 3 pounds)

4 large eggs

¼ teaspoon salt, plus more to taste

¼ teaspoon ground white pepper, plus more to taste

¼ cup vegetable or peanut oil

1 cup fresh or thawed frozen green peas or shelled edamame

½ cup finely diced carrots

4 cups cooked white rice (preferably day-old rice)

2 tablespoons Fried Shallots (see page 52)

2 whole scallions, trimmed and finely chopped

Bring a large pot of water deep enough to submerge the crab to a boil. Drop in the crab and cover. Cook for 20 minutes (for a 3-pound crab). Drain and cool for several minutes. Once cool enough to handle, pull off the claws and legs and crack open using seafood crackers. Reserve the meat in a bowl and discard the shells. Pull off the top shell of the crab and set aside for serving. Pick out the shoulder meat from the crab and reserve in the bowl of crabmeat.

Beat the eggs with the salt and white pepper. Heat 1 tablespoon of the oil in a large skillet or wok over medium-high heat. Once hot, pour in the eggs and stir immediately to break up the pieces. Once scrambled, about 30 seconds, transfer to a dish and set aside. Heat another tablespoon of the oil and, once hot, toss in the peas or edamame and carrots. Cook, stirring occasionally, until the carrots are lightly softened and the peas are bright green, about 2 minutes. Remove from the pan and set aside.

Heat the remaining 2 tablespoons oil and add the rice. Season generously with pinches of salt and white pepper and cook, stirring with a spatula to break apart any chunks, about 1 minute. Return the eggs, peas, and carrots to the pan and add the fried shallots. Stir to combine thoroughly. Taste for seasoning, adding salt and white pepper as desired. Remove from the heat and stir in the reserved crabmeat and the scallions. Give a final toss to incorporate throughout and transfer to a serving dish. Serve with the reserved top of the crab shell for decoration.

Desserts and Drinks

Peanut Mochi (page 247)

Pineapple Tarts (Feng Li Su)

鳳梨酥

Makes about 12

With square, buttery crusts encasing a jammy pineapple filling, this pastry is a unique Taiwanese treat. You'll find them sold as if they were fine truffles throughout Taiwan, wrapped in fancy boxes and packaging. No one can resist them once they've tried just one, so a box of these is a popular gift item, and a must-have souvenir when traveling. Because of their neat, square shape, it's not exactly easy to make pineapple tarts at home. But warm and freshly baked, they're well worth the effort.

For the filling	For the crust
1 medium pineapple	2½ sticks (1¼ cups) cold unsalted butter
1 cup water	1½ cups all-purpose flour, plus more for dusting
1 cup sugar	½ cup cornstarch
	2 tablespoons sugar
	½ teaspoon salt
	¼ teaspoon baking powder
	1 to 2 tablespoons cold water

For the filling

Trim the fronds and base from the pineapple and cut off the tough skin. Slice lengthwise in half and then into quarters. Cut the thick center core from each quarter. Chop the remaining pineapple. Place in a saucepan along with the water and sugar and bring just to a boil. Reduce the heat to a simmer and cook, uncovered, stirring occasionally, until the liquid has been reduced to a jamlike consistency and the color has turned a deeper, more orange color, about 1 hour. Continue to simmer, stirring occasionally, until the mixture is dry enough to pick up with your hand and roll into a ball, about 2 hours. Let cool completely.

For the crust

Cut the butter into small cubes. In a separate bowl, combine the flour, cornstarch, sugar, salt, and baking powder. Cut the butter into the dry ingredients using a pastry cutter or your hands until the mixture resembles coarse crumbs, with pieces of butter no larger than peas. Sprinkle in the water a little at a time, just enough until the mixture comes together in a ball. Form the dough into two balls and cover with plastic wrap. Refrigerate for 30 minutes.

Preheat the oven to 350°F. Cut each ball of dough into 6 equal-sized pieces. Flatten one piece against a lightly floured surface into a 3-inch round. Place 1 heaping teaspoon of the pineapple filling in the center of the round. Carefully bring the edges of the dough to the center to seal it shut over the filling. Place seam-side down on a lightly floured surface, and press the ball down gently to flatten the top. Gently press the sides of the ball with a scraper or flat knife to form a rough rectangle. Repeat with the remaining dough and pineapple filling.

Arrange the tarts at least 1 inch apart on an ungreased cookie sheet. Bake until the tops are pale golden brown, about 30 minutes. Transfer to a wire rack to cool before serving.

Crushed Ice with Mangoes and Syrup (Mang Guo Bao Bing)

芒果刨冰

Makes about 4 servings

There are numerous iterations of this shaved ice dessert in Taiwan—often with fresh fruit, but also with additions of tapioca pearls, sweetened red beans, or chunks of taro root or sweet potatoes in syrup. Many shops specializing in these icy desserts allow customers to create their own sundaelike creation. My favorite one focuses on mangoes, which are always juicy and flavorful, grown locally on the tropical island. A touch of sweetened condensed milk poured over the ensemble adds creamy richness to an otherwise light treat.

1 cup mango juice

1 cup water

¼ cup sugar

1 large ripe mango, peeled, pitted, and diced

4 cups ice cubes, gently crushed

1 (8-ounce) can sweetened condensed milk

Combine the mango juice, water, and sugar in a saucepan. Bring to a boil, stirring, to dissolve the sugar. Continue to cook at a rapid boil until the mixture reduces by almost half, about 15 minutes. Let cool completely and then refrigerate until cold, about 1 hour. Toss the mango with the syrup.

Place the ice in a blender and pulse several times, stopping to scrape down the sides occasionally. Once the mixture resembles fine crumbles, transfer to individual serving dishes (discard any large chunks of ice). Top each dish with a generous scoop of the mangoes in syrup. Top each with a drizzle of the sweetened condensed milk and serve immediately.

Note

If you have an old-fashioned ice shaver at home, you can use this to create the classic texture of this crushed ice. But you can use a blender to crush the ice into coarser, crushed bits. To eliminate large chunks, it's best to use your refrigerator's ice crusher setting, if available, before placing the ice in the blender.

Crushed Ice Milk with Fruit Toppings (Shui Guo Niu Nai Bing)

水果牛奶冰

Makes about 4 servings

The shaved ice and topping dessert trend in Taiwan has spurned this smart variation, which features frozen milk that's shaved or crushed instead of ice. Often called "snow ice" in Taiwanese dessert shops, the milk shavings are snowy white and creamy tasting. Again, the proper ice-shaving appliances would be ideal when making this, but I've made it work by filling up ice cube trays only halfway with milk, then transferring the small cubes to a blender once frozen. It takes several pulses to become coarse, somewhat uniform crumbles. But as it melts, this icy "snow" will soften.

4 cups whole milk

1 cup water

¼ cup sugar

2 to 4 cups coarsely chopped fresh fruit, such as strawberries, kiwis, and/or mangoes

4 scoops assorted ice cream or sorbet

Pour the milk into ice cube trays and freeze overnight. Combine the water and sugar in a saucepan. Bring to a boil, stirring, to dissolve the sugar. Continue to cook at a rapid boil until the mixture reduces by almost half, about 15 minutes. Let cool completely and then refrigerate until cold, about 1 hour. Toss the syrup with the fruit of your choice.

Place the frozen milk cubes in a blender and pulse several times, stopping to scrape down the sides occasionally. Once the mixture resembles fine crumbles, transfer to a large serving platter (discard any large chunks). Scatter the chopped fruit in syrup across the snow and top with the scoops of ice cream. Serve immediately.

Crushed Ice with Mangoes and Syrup (page 232)

Crushed Ice Milk
with Fruit Toppings
(page 233)

Tapioca Pearl Tea (Zhen Zhu Nai Cha)

珍珠奶茶

Makes 2 servings

Iced tea with tapioca pearls that are sucked from a large straw is perhaps Taiwan's most famous culinary export. These bouncy, chewy balls of tapioca are fun to munch on, much like chewing gum. The teas may be milky or not, sweetened or not, and flavored with any number of additional powders or infusions, like mango. My favorite style is this classic black tea with milk, and sweetened.

1 cup tapioca pearls
(found in the dry goods section in Asian groceries)

4 cups freshly brewed strong black tea

1 tablespoon sugar

Ice cubes, for shaking

½ cup whole milk

Soak the tapioca pearls according to the package instructions. Once fully reconstituted and softened, drain.

While the tea is still hot or warm, add the sugar and stir to dissolve completely. Let cool and then refrigerate until completely chilled, about 2 hours, before serving.

Place the tapioca pearls at the bottom of 2 cups. Use a cocktail shaker to shake together the ice, milk, and tea and strain into each cup and serve.

Taiwanese Tea Culture

Atop the mountain range overlooking Taipei, the village of Maokong is home to centuries-old tea farms, and along with it, a tradition of using tea to flavor other foods. There are thirteen major tea-growing regions throughout Taiwan, all situated on mountain ranges. Each region produces their specific type of high-mountain tea, which is enjoyed greatly by the Taiwanese and tea connoisseurs far and wide.

A traditional tea service

Tea leaves in a bamboo scoop / Pouring oolong tea

Tea has been grown commercially in Taiwan from the eighteenth century on, after Chinese settlers found its extensive mountains exceptional for growing oolong tea leaves. Unlike most garden crops, tea develops character from growing in difficult conditions, such as mountainous terrain. After harvesting, the leaves are then treated to a number of different fermenting, aging, roasting, and other processing styles, creating unique flavors that are best compared with the making of distinctive regional wines.

Enjoying tea is certainly rooted in tradition in Taiwan; the Chinese and Japanese tea ceremonies have not been forgotten, and many teahouses specialize in this ritualized service and observance of tea drinking in Taiwan. In modern times, teas have branched out in myriad styles and preparations to suit the tastes of an ever-evolving Taiwanese culture. For example, it's iced or chilled, served with fruits and juices, or dessertlike additions like cold pudding or tapioca pearls (see page 237) for a refreshing drink. In recent decades also, it has spurred a wave of cafés offering tea-infused snacks and dishes, as found in Maokong and other tea-farming areas.

The recipes for tea-sprinkled fried rice (see page 94) and shrimp (see page 204) were inspired by my visits to these regions in Taiwan. With their floral, yet toasty and savory notes, crushed tea leaves make an exciting topping, along with chopped fresh herbs, on almost anything. Tea leaves are sometimes added to stocks, stews, and braises in Taiwan for a deep color as well as a hint of herbal flavor, such as in the recipe for tea eggs (see page 85). I wish that I could have included recipes for the dishes I'd tried that were flavored with tea seed oil. This condiment can be found sold at tiny gift stores around tea-growing regions in Taiwan, and shares a deeply nutty flavor and rich aroma with toasted sesame oil. It's a different flavor, but similarly robust, and as such the oil is often used to garnish dishes, like the simple noodles scented with sesame oil and ginger (see page 156). However, Taiwanese tea seed oil is not something one can find easily in conventional stores even in Taiwan—let alone outside the island—for it's primarily sold at souvenir shops in tea-growing regions.

However, with garnishing and braising with tea leaves firmly established in these regions, I imagine that this "tea cuisine" will only continue to proliferate in creativity. It's an exciting time to watch how this happens, and to try experimenting with the recipes oneself. Given that tea is so steeped in Taiwanese culture, and is such an important part of its agricultural heritage, one can only imagine all the ways that tea will manifest in Taiwanese cuisine. We may have yet to experience the full scope of flavors and possibilities for this proud national product.

Hakka-Style Sweet Green Tea (Ke Jia Lei Cha)

客家擂茶

Makes about 4 servings

Traditions of the Hakka people are well maintained on Taiwan. This uniquely flavorful tea is enjoyed by Taiwanese of all backgrounds in tea shops and cafés throughout Taiwan today. One can purchase a preblended mixture of its ingredients—which include crushed peanuts, toasted rice, and sesame seeds—to steep easily in a teapot. Or, you can blend the ingredients yourself. It's deliciously savory, sort of like having your breakfast cereal and tea in one cup.

½ cup loose green tea leaves

¼ cup roasted, unsalted, shelled peanuts

¼ cup toasted sesame seeds

¼ cup puffed rice cereal

2 cups boiling water

Gently crush the tea leaves in a mortar and pestle. Transfer to another dish, and gently crush the peanuts in the mortar and pestle. Transfer the peanuts to the dish with the tea leaves, and gently crush the sesame seeds in the mortar and pestle. Combine the tea, peanuts, sesame seeds, and cereal in a teapot. Fill with the boiling water and cover the pot. Let steep for 2 to 3 minutes and then serve immediately.

Fresh Watermelon Shake (Xi Gua Bing Sha)

西瓜冰沙

Makes 2 servings

The hot, tropical climate in Taiwan is very kind to fruits that thrive on sunshine. If you thought that watermelon, honeydew, and other melons were boring and bland-tasting, you've got to try the ones grown in Taiwan. Because it's so warm, fresh, cool fruit juices are sold everywhere on the island. I drink a tall glass of watermelon juice practically every day that I spend in Taiwan, sometimes two. This is one fruit that can be readily found at the height of summer in the States, and produces plenty of juice to blend up.

1 cup water

1 tablespoon sugar

4 cups cold, seedless watermelon, cut into chunks

Ice cubes (optional)

Heat the water in a small saucepan over medium heat and stir in the sugar. Continue heating, stirring until the sugar just dissolves. Transfer to a separate dish and cool completely.

Combine the sugar solution and the watermelon in a blender and puree thoroughly. Pour into serving cups, with ice if desired, and serve immediately.

Brown Sugar Cake (Heitang Gao)

黑糖糕

Makes about 12 servings

This fluffy, loaf-shaped cake is a specialty of Taiwan's Penghu Islands. It's believed that it was first sold by a Japanese-owned bakery during the Japanese occupation, when Western-style cakes and sweet desserts were a novelty in Taiwan. Nowadays, this famous cake can be found in bakeries throughout Taiwan, which offer an array of Western and Japanese-style pastries, cookies, and cakes. Since most Taiwanese households do not have an oven, however, the cake is typically steamed. This gives the cake its spongy moistness and cooks it thoroughly. It's a little difficult to find a steamer or double-boiler that will fit a standard loaf pan inside and still close completely. If you're at a loss for this setup, just pour the batter into small ramekins instead to make single-serving miniature cakes.

1½ cups all-purpose flour

½ cup rice flour

2 teaspoons baking powder

1 teaspoon baking soda

¼ teaspoon salt

3 large eggs

¾ cup packed dark brown sugar, plus about 2 tablespoons for the pan

½ cup whole milk

¼ cup vegetable or peanut oil

1 tablespoon unsalted butter or oil for greasing the pan

1 tablespoon toasted sesame seeds

Prepare a steamer or double boiler that's large enough to fit the loaf pan inside (or use a very large, wide stockpot or Dutch oven). Place at least four cups of water at the bottom, and make sure that the cake pan can be elevated with a steamer rack so that the cake pan doesn't touch the water.

Sift together both flours, the baking powder, baking soda, and salt in a large bowl.

In another large bowl, beat the eggs and stir in the ¾ cup brown sugar. Whisk until fluffy. Whisk in the milk and oil. While whisking, gradually add the dry ingredients until thoroughly incorporated with no lumps.

Heat the steamer so that the water is boiling. Grease the loaf pan with the butter. Sprinkle the remaining 2 tablespoons brown sugar all around the interior. Pour the batter into the pan. Place in the steamer, cover, and steam until a toothpick inserted into the center of the cake comes out clean, about 30 minutes. Remove carefully from the steamer and immediately sprinkle the top with the sesame seeds. Let cool for at least 5 minutes before carefully removing from the mold. Cool on a wire rack for another 5 minutes before slicing.

Peanut Mochi (Hua Sheng Ma Ji)

花生麻糬

Makes 16

Several of Taiwan's aboriginal tribes produce chewy, sticky, sweet filling–stuffed mochi using millet flour, a staple grain in these communities. They're surprisingly similar to mochi made with glutinous rice flour, as is typical throughout the rest of Taiwan (and in China and Japan). Perhaps not surprisingly, mochi is pretty tricky to make at home. The dough is testy to handle, especially when it comes to filling the centers. But mochi is so enjoyed in Taiwan that I had to try making it for friends. Of all the different flavors I tried, the peanut-filled mochi were most enjoyed around the room. Fortunately, they were also the easiest ones to make, as the stiffer ground peanut paste stayed separate from the sticky dough when shaping into balls.

For the filling

2 cups roasted, unsalted, shelled peanuts

½ cup brown sugar

For the mochi

2 cups glutinous rice flour (sweet rice flour)

½ cup cold water

1 cup boiling water

Vegetable or peanut oil, for greasing

1 cup cornstarch, for dusting

For the filling

Combine the peanuts and sugar in a food processor. Pulse several times, scraping down the sides, until the mixture becomes pastelike with some irregular chunks. Set aside.

For the mochi

Preheat the oven to 300°F. Bring a saucepan of water to a boil. Place the glutinous flour in a bowl, and stir in the cold water until the mixture just forms a paste. While stirring rapidly, pour the boiling water into the rice flour mixture and continue stirring until the mixture is thick and gluey. Lightly grease an 8-by-8-inch casserole with the oil, and transfer the batter to the dish. Cover with foil and bake until the mochi feels soft and springy to the touch, and no longer coats your finger with goop, about 30 minutes.

Allow to cool completely, about 1 hour. Spread the cornstarch on a work surface and carefully invert the dish, scraping the mochi out with the help of a spatula if needed. Cut into 16 pieces. Gently pull and stretch a piece to flatten it slightly and place about a tablespoon of the peanut paste in the center. Carefully stretch the mochi around the peanut paste to cover entirely and seal shut. Roll the completed mochi in the cornstarch and set aside. Repeat with the remaining mochi pieces and filling. Serve within 2 days. Store in an airtight container at room temperature.

Sweet Tofu Custard (Tian Dou Hua)

甜豆花

Makes 4 to 6 servings

A popular sweet street food, this tofu is even softer than the softest silken tofu. That's because it's not really tofu, but rather soybean milk that's set ever so gently with a solidifying agent. Typically, this would be gypsum powder, which can be found in Asian markets. But I've managed to achieve a soft set using unflavored gelatin, which is more easily found in the States. Its name in Chinese—dou hua—literally translates to "bean flower," because it's so delicate. Swimming in syrup and often topped with sweet baubles like red beans or tapioca pearls by street vendors, it's adored by kids, but it's also quite healthy as far as desserts go. Here, I've made a ginger-infused syrup in which to submerge the clouds of tofu custard.

For the tofu custard

1 quart unsweetened
or lightly sweetened soy milk

½ cup warm water

1 tablespoon unflavored gelatin

For the syrup

2 cups water

1 (2-inch) piece fresh ginger,
peeled and sliced into 8 to 10 thick discs

½ cup sugar

For the tofu custard

Heat the soy milk in a large pot over medium-high heat until it just reaches a boil, turning off the heat as soon as the first bubbles emerge around the sides.

In a medium bowl, stir together the warm water and gelatin until the gelatin is thoroughly dissolved. While whisking, slowly pour in about 1 cup of the hot soy milk. Continue whisking and pour in another cup of the soy milk. Transfer the gelatin mixture to the remaining soy milk in the pot and whisk to incorporate thoroughly. Let the soy milk mixture cool completely. Cover and refrigerate for at least 4 hours (or overnight).

For the syrup

Combine the water, ginger, and sugar in a small pot. Bring just to a boil, stirring to dissolve the sugar. Reduce the heat to a simmer and cook, uncovered, until the syrup has reduced and thickened slightly, about 15 minutes. Strain and remove the ginger.

Scoop out large chunks of the chilled tofu custard to serve in individual bowls drizzled with the syrup.

Food of Taiwan

Page numbers in *italics* indicate photos.

A

Aboriginal tribes, 18, 21, *26*, 27, 29, 39
Agriculture, *16–17*, 35, *36–37*
    aboriginal, 39
    crops, *35*, 35
    and land reform, 23
    tea growing, *24*, 35, 239–240, *241*
Anusasananan, Linda Lau, 29
Appetizers/street food snacks. *See also* Buns
    Burrito, Taiwanese (Run Bing), 94, *95*
    Chicken Bites, Fried (Yan Su Ji), 86, *87*
    Coffin Cake (Guan Cai Ban), *78–79*, 79
    Corn, Grilled, Taiwanese (Kao Yu Mi), 88, *89*
    lu wei (braised food), 82, *83*
    Meatball Mochi (Ba-Wan), 90, *91*
    in night markets, *80–81*, 81–82, *83*
    Oyster Omelet (E Zai Jian // O Ah Jian), 76, *77*
    Pot Stickers, Pork and Napa Cabbage, Pan-Fried (Guotie), 73–75, *74*, *75*
    Shrimp Rolls, Deep-Fried (Xia Juan), 225
    Sticky Rice, Molded (Tong Zai Mi Gao), *92*, 93
    stinky tofu, 123–124, *125*
    Tea Eggs (Cha Ye Dan), *84*, 85

B

Bamboo Shoots
    Chicken Soup with Mushrooms and (Zhu Sun Ji Tang), 160, *161*
    fresh, preparing, 159
BaoHaus bun shop, New York, 18
Basil
    Clams (Ta Xiang Ge Li), *218*, 219
    Eggplant, Braised, with Garlic and (Jiu Ceng Ta Qie Zi), 101
    Thai, fresh, 44, *45*
    Bean Sauce, Fermented, Noodles with Minced Pork and (Zha Jiang Mian), 154–155, *155*
Bean Sprouts, Stir-Fried Beef with Pickled Mustard Greens and (Zha Cai Niu Rou Si), 189
Beef
    Noodle Soup, Taiwanese (Niu Rou Mian), 15, 132–133, *133*, 136
    Sha-Cha Stir-Fried, with Watercress, (Sha Cha Niu Rou Kong Xin Cai), *190–191*, 192
    Stir-Fried, with Pickled Mustard Greens and Bean Sprouts (Zha Cai Niu Rou Si), 189
Bento boxes, Taiwanese, *172*, 173–174

Beverages
    Tea, Sweet Green, Hakka-Style (Ke Jia Lei Cha), *242*, 243
    Tea, Tapioca Pearl (Zhen Zhu Nai Cha), *236*, 237
    Watermelon Shake, Fresh (Xi Gua Bing Sha), *244*, 245
Bitter Melon
    Chicken and Pineapple Soup (Ku Gua Feng Li Ji Tang), 162, *163*
    Stuffed (Niang Ku Gua), 113, *114*
Black Beans, Fermented, 43
    Black Bean Sauce, Oysters with (Yin Chi E Zai // Yin Xi O Ah), 214, *215*
    Okra with Garlic, Chilies and (Dou Chao Qiu Kui), *115*, 116
Black Vinegar, Chilled Oysters with Cilantro, Shallots and (Cong Xiag Xian E // Cong Xian Xian Ke), 217
Bok Choy
    in Noodles with Minced Pork and Fermented Bean Sauce (Zha Jiang Mian), 154–155, *155*
    in Oyster Omelet (E Zai Jian // O Ah Jian), 76, *77*
Brown Sugar Cake (Heitang Gao), 246
Buddhism, 82
Buns
    Daikon Radish Pastries, Flaky (Luo Bo Si Bing), *64–65*, 72
    Leek, with Dried Shrimp, Pan-Fried (Jiu Cai Shui Jian Bao), 70–71
    Pork Belly, Taiwanese (Gua Bao), 18, 66, 67
    Pork, Peppery (Hua Jiao Bin), 68–69
Burrito, Taiwanese (Run Bing), 94, *95*

C

Cabbage
    Braised, with Dried Shrimp and Shiitake Mushrooms (Lu Bai Cai), 105, *107*
    in Burrito, Taiwanese (Run Bing), 94, *95*
    Napa, in Noodles with Minced Pork and Fermented Bean Sauce (Zha Jiang Mian), 154–155, *155*
    Napa, and Pork Pot Stickers, Pan-Fried (Guotie), 73–75, *74*, *75*
    Napa, and Shredded Pork Stew (Xi Lu Rou), 196, *197*
    Vinegar-Pickled (Suan Cai), 59, 61
Cake
    Brown Sugar (Heitang Gao), 246
    Coffin (Guan Cai Ban), *78–79*, 79
Chen, Jade and Muriel, 18
Chen Jingyi, 18
Chen Shui-bian, 11, 13, 15, 23

Chen Yi, 23
Chiang Kai-shek, 13, 23
Chicken
    Bites, Fried (Yan Su Ji), 86, *87*
    in Burrito, Taiwanese (Run Bing), 94, *95*
    in Coffin Cake (Guan Cai Ban), *78–79*, 79
    Noodles, Chilled, with Sesame Sauce and (Liang Mian), 157
    Pineapple and Bitter Melon Soup (Ku Gua Feng Li Ji Tang), 162, *163*
    Shredded, over Rice (Ji Rou Fan), 176
    Soup with Bamboo Shoots and Mushrooms (Zhu Sun Ji Tang), 160, *161*
    Steaks, Fried (Zha Ji Pai), 170, *171*
    Three Cup (San Bei Ji), *168*, 169
    Wine-Stewed, with Sesame Oil (Ma You Ji), 177, *178*
Chili bean sauce, 43
Chilies
    dried, in Sha-Cha Sauce (Sha Cha Jiang), 47, 53
    Eggplant, Steamed, with Garlic and (Suan Rong Qie) Zi, 102, *103*
    Okra with Garlic, Fermented Black Beans and (Dou Chao Qiu Kui), *115*, 116
    varieties of, 44, *45*
Chili oil, ma-la, 44
Chili sauce, fresh, 44, *45*
China-Taiwan trade, 15
Chingye Shinleyuan restaurant, Taiwan, 18
Chives, Yellow, Stir-Fried Slivered Pork with (Jiu Huang Rou Si), 187
Cilantro, 43
    Fish, Pan-Fried, with Peanuts and (Xiang Jian Yu Pai), 211
    Oysters, Chilled, with Black Vinegar, Shallots and (Cong Xiag Xian E // Cong Xian Xian Ke), 217
Citrus and Soy-Based Sauce, Sweet-and-Sour (Yang Sheng Zhan Jiang), 55
Clam(s)
    Basil (Ta Xiang Ge Li), *218*, 219
    Braised with Loofah Squash (Ge Li Si Gua), 221
    and Daikon Radish Soup (Ge Li Luo Buo Tang), 158
    Egg Noodles, Pan-Fried, with Seafood (Hai Xian Chao Mian), 148
    Wine-Marinated (Yan Ge Li // Xin Ha Ma), 220, *222*
Climate, 33
Cod, Steamed, with Five-Flavor Sauce (Wu Wei Yu), 208, *209*
Coffin Cake (Guan Cai Ban), *78–79*, 79

Condiments
  Cabbage, Vinegar-Pickled (Suan Cai), *59*, 61
  Cucumbers, Spicy Marinated (Suan La Xiao Huang Gua), 63
  Cucumbers, Sweet Soy-Pickled (Yan Xiao Huang Gua), 62
  Dipping Sauce, Dumpling (Jiaozi Jiang), 56
  Mustard Greens, Pickled (Zha Cai), *50*, 57, *58*
  Mustard Greens Relish, Pickled (Xue Cai), 60
  pantry staples, 41, 43, 44, 47
  Peanut Powder, Crushed (Hua Sheng Fen), 43, 63
  Sha-Cha Sauce (Sha Cha Jiang), 47, 53
  Shallots, Fried (Hong Cong Tou), 52
  Sweet-and-Sour Citrus and Soy-Based Sauce (Yang Sheng Zhan Jiang), 55
  Sweet-and-Sour Tomato-Based Sauce (Hai Shan Jiang), 54
  tea seed oil, 240
Congee, Sweet Potato (Di Gua Xi Fan), 164, *165*
Corn
  in Coffin Cake (Guan Cai Ban), 78–79, *79*
  Grilled, Taiwanese (Kao Yu Mi), 88, *89*
Cornstarch, 43
Crab Fried Rice (Xie Rou Chao Fan), 227
Cross-Strait Service Trade Agreement, 15
Cucumbers
  Soy-Pickled, Sweet (Yan Xiao Huang Gua), 62
  Spicy Marinated (Suan La Xiao Huang Gua), 63
Custard, Tofu, Sweet (Tian Dou Hua), *248*, 249

D
Daikon Radish
  and Clam Soup (Ge Li Luo Buo Tang), 158
  Omelet, Dried Radish (Cai Fu Dan), 98, *99*
  Pastries, Flaky (Luo Bo Si Bing), 64–65, 72
Danzai Noodle Soup (Dan Zai Mian), 138, *139*
Date Sauce, Pan-Fried Tofu with (Gan Mei Dou Fu), 120, *121*
Democratic Progressive Party, 11, 13, 15, 23
Desserts
  Brown Sugar Cake (Heitang Gao), 246
  Ice, Crushed, with Mangoes and Syrup (Mang Guo Bao Bing), 232, *234*
  Ice Milk, Crushed, with Fruit Toppings (Shui Guo Niu Nai Bing), 233, *235*
  Peanut Mochi (Hua Sheng Ma Ji), *228*, 247
  Pineapple Tarts (Feng Li Su), 230–231, *231*
  Tofu Custard, Sweet (Tian Dou Hua), *248*, 249
Din Tai Fung restaurant, 136, *137*
Dip, Ginger-Soy, Tomato Salad with (Liang Ban Fan Qie), 100
Dipping Sauce, Dumpling (Jiaozi Jiang), 56

Dragon Beard Fern, 39
  Ohitashi (Liang Ban Long Xu Cai), *96–97*, 112
Dumpling Dipping Sauce (Jiaozi Jiang), 56
Dumplings, 11
  Meatball Mochi (Ba-Wan), *90*, 91, 136
  Pot Stickers, Pork and Napa Cabbage, Pan-Fried (Guotie), 73–75, *74*, *75*
  soup, 136, *137*
Dutch East India Company, 21

E
Economic growth, 23
Edamame
  Dry Tofu with (Dou Gan Chao Mao Dou Ren), *118*, 119
  in Noodles with Minced Pork and Fermented Bean Sauce (Zha Jiang Mian), 154–155, *155*
Egg Noodles, Pan-Fried, with Seafood (Hai Xian Chao Mian), 148
Eggplant
  Braised, with Garlic and Basil (Jiu Ceng Ta Qie Zi), 101
  Steamed, with Garlic and Chilies (Suan Rong Qie) Zi, 102, *103*
Eggs
  Omelet, Oyster (E Zai Jian // O Ah Jian), 76, 77
  Omelet, Radish, Dried (Cai Fu Dan), 98, *99*
  Scrambled, in Burrito, Taiwanese (Run Bing), 94, *95*
  Tea Eggs (Cha Ye Dan), *84*, 85

F
Fish. *See also* Seafood
  balls/cakes, commercially available, 204
  balls/cakes, texture of, 203–204
  Cod, Steamed, with Five-Flavor Sauce (Wu Wei Yu), 208, *209*
  dried, in Sha-Cha Sauce (Sha Cha Jiang), 47, 53
  fishcakes, *202–203*
  Fishcakes, Fried (Tian Bu La), *200*, 201
  Pan-Fried, with Peanuts and Cilantro (Xiang Jian Yu Pai), 211
  Pan-Fried Whole, with Garlic, Ginger, and Scallions (Cong Jiang Quan Yu), 206, *207*
  paste, 204
  Spanish Mackerel Noodle Soup (Tu Tun Yu Geng Mian), 145
Fishing industry, 35
Five-Flavor Sauce, Steamed Cod with (Wu Wei Yu), 208, *209*

Five-spice powder, 44, *45*
Fort Zeelandia, Siege of, 22
Fruit Toppings, Crushed Ice Milk with (Shui Guo Niu Nai Bing), 233, *235*

G
Garlic
  Eggplant, Braised, with Basil and (Jiu Ceng Ta Qie Zi), 101
  Eggplant, Steamed, with Chilies and (Suan Rong Qie) Zi, 102, *103*
  Fish, Pan-Fried Whole, with Ginger, Scallions and (Cong Jiang Quan Yu), 206, *207*
  Okra with Chilies, Fermented Black Beans and (Dou Chao Qiu Kui), *115*, 116
  Sweet Potato Leaves with, Sautéed (Suan Rong Fan Shu Ye), *108*, 109
Geography and climate, *32*, 33, *34*, 35, 38–*39*
Ginger, 44
  Fish, Pan-Fried Whole, with Garlic, Scallions and (Cong Jiang Quan Yu), 206, *207*
  King Oyster Mushrooms with, Sautéed (Qing Chao Xing Bao Gu), 104, *106*
  Soy Dip, Tomato Salad with (Liang Ban Fan Qie), 100
"Gourmet powder", 44
Green Tea, Sweet, Hakka-Style (Ke Jia Lei Cha), *242*, 243

H
Hakka people, 18, 29
Hakka-Style Pork Stir-Fry (Ke Jia Xiao Chao), *185*, 186
Hakka-Style Sweet Green Tea (Ke Jia Lei Cha), *242*, 243
Hokkien dialect, 15, 18
Hoklo people, 27
Huang, Eddie, 18

I
Ice, Crushed, with Mangoes and Syrup (Mang Guo Bao Bing), 232, *234*
Ice Milk, Crushed, with Fruit Toppings (Shui Guo Niu Nai Bing), 233, *235*
Immigration from mainland China, 13, 22, 23, 27, 135–136
Ingredients in Taiwanese cuisine, 41, 43, 44, *45*, 47

J

Japan, occupation of Taiwan, 22–23, 174

K

King Oyster Mushrooms, Sautéed, with Ginger (Qing Chao Xing Bao Gu), 104, *106*
Koxinga (Zheng Chenggong), *22, 22*
Kuomintang, 11, 13, 14, 15, 23

L

Land reform, 23
Language, 15, 18
Leek Buns with Dried Shrimp, Pan-Fried (Jiu Cai Shui Jian Bao), 70–71
Lee Teng-hui, 23
Liver, Pan-Fried Pork, with Sweet and Sour Glaze (Jian Zhu Gan), 193
Loofah Squash, Clams Braised with (Ge Li Si Gua), 221
Lu wei (braised street snack foods), 82, *83*

M

Mackerel, Spanish, Noodle Soup (Tu Tun Yu Geng Mian), 145
Ma-la chili oil, 44
Mandarin language, 15
Mangoes, Crushed Ice with Syrup and (Mang Guo Bao Bing), 232, *234*
Mao Zedong, 13, 23
Ma Ying-jeou, 13, 23
Meatball(s)
    commercially available, 203
    Mochi (Ba-Wan), 90, *91*
    Pork, Rice Noodles in Thick Soup with (Rou Geng/Ba Kinn), 82, *126*, 130–131
    texture of, 203–204
Melon
    Bitter, Chicken and Pineapple Soup (Ku Gua Feng Li Ji Tang), 162, *163*
    Bitter, Stuffed (Niang Ku Gua), 113, *114*
    Watermelon Shake, Fresh (Xi Gua Bing Sha), 244, *245*
    Winter, Crispy Spareribs Soup with (Pai Gu Su Tang), 150–151
Military villages (juan cun), *134–135*, 136–137
Ming Dynasty, 21, *22, 22*
Mochi
    Meatball (Ba-Wan), 90, *91*
    Peanut (Hua Sheng Ma Ji), *228*, 247
Mushrooms. *See also* Shiitake Mushrooms, Dried
    Chicken Soup with Bamboo Shoots and (Zhu Sun Ji Tang), 159

King Oyster, Sautéed, with Ginger (Qing Chao Xing Bao Gu), 104, *106*
Mustard Greens
    Pickled (Zha Cai), *50*, 57, *58*
    Pickled, Stir-Fried Beef with Bean Sprouts and (Zha Cai Niu Rou Si), 189
    Relish, Pickled (Xue Cai), 60

N

Napa Cabbage
    in Burrito, Taiwanese (Run Bing), 94, *95*
    in Noodles with Minced Pork and Fermented Bean Sauce (Zha Jiang Mian), 154–155, *155*
    and Pork Pot Stickers, Pan-Fried (Guotie), 73–75, *74, 75*
    and Shredded Pork Stew (Xi Lu Rou), 196, *197*
Night markets, *80–81*, 81–82
Noodles
    Chilled, with Chicken and Sesame Sauce (Liang Mian), 157
    Pan-Fried Egg Noodles with Seafood (Hai Xian Chao Mian), 148
    Pan-Fried Rice Noodles with Pork and Vegetables (Chao Mi Fen), *152*, 153
    with Pork, Minced, and Fermented Bean Sauce (Zha Jiang Mian), 154–155, *155*
    rice noodles, dried, 43
    Sesame-Scented Thin (Ma You Mian Xian), *156*, 156
Noodle Soup(s)
    Beef, Taiwanese (Niu Rou Mian), 15, 132–133, *133*, 136
    Danzai (Dan Zai Mian), 138, *139*
    Oyster (E Zai Mian Xian // O Ah Mi Suan), 140, *142–143*
    Pork Chop, Fried, 146–147, *147*
    Spanish Mackerel (Tu Tun Yu Geng Mian), 145
    Thick, Rice Noodles in, with Pork Meatballs (Rou Geng/Ba Kinn), 82, *126*, 130–131

O

Okra with Garlic, Chilies and Fermented Black Beans (Dou Chao Qiu Kui), *115*, 116
Omelet
    Oyster (E Zai Jian // O Ah Jian), 76, 77
    Radish, Dried (Cai Fu Dan), 98, *99*
Organic farming, 39

Oyster(s)
    with Black Bean Sauce (Yin Chi E Zai // Yin Xi O Ah), 214, *215*
    Chilled, with Black Vinegar, Cilantro, and Shallots (Cong Xiag Xian E // Cong Xian Xian Ke), 217
    Fried (E Zai Su // O Ah So), 216
    fritters, *141*
    Noodle Soup (E Zai Mian Xian// O Ah Mi Suan), 140, *142–143*
    Omelet (E Zai Jian // O Ah Jian), 76, 77
Oyster Mushrooms, King, Sautéed, with Ginger (Qing Chao Xing Bao Gu), 104, *106*

P

Pantry staples, 41, 43, 44, 47
Pastries
    Daikon Radish, Flaky (Luo Bo Si Bing), *64–65*, 72
    Tarts, Pineapple (Feng Li Su), 230–231, *231*
Peanut(s)
    Mochi (Hua Sheng Ma Ji, *228*, 247
    Pan-Fried Fish with Cilantro and (Xiang Jian Yu Pai), 211
    Powder, Crushed (Hua Sheng Fen), 43, 63
Pepper, white, 47
Peppery Pork Buns (Hua Jiao Bin), 68–69
Pickles, Pickled
    Cabbage, Vinegar- (Suan Cai), 59, 61
    Cucumbers, Sweet Soy- (Yan Xiao Huang Gua), 62
    Mustard Greens (Zha Cai), *50*, 57, *58*
    Mustard Greens Relish (Xue Cai), 60
    Mustard Greens, Stir-Fried Beef with Bean Sprouts and (Zha Cai Niu Rou Si), 189
    with Pork, Steamed Ground (Gua Zai Rou), 188
Pig's Knuckle, Red-Braised (Hong Shao Zhu Jiao), 182
Pineapple
    Chicken and Bitter Melon Soup (Ku Gua Feng Li Ji Tang), 162, *163*
    Tarts (Feng Li Su), 230–231, *231*
Population, 29
Pork
    in Bitter Melon, Stuffed (Niang Ku Gua), 113, *114*
    Buns, Peppery Pork (Hua Jiao Bin), 68–69
    Buns, Pork Belly, Taiwanese (Gua Bao), 18, 66, *67*
    in Burrito, Taiwanese (Run Bing), 94, *95*
    Liver, Pan-Fried, with Sweet and Sour Glaze (Jian Zhu Gan), 193
    Meatball Mochi (Ba-Wan), 90, *91*

Meatballs, Rice Noodles in Thick Soup with (Rou Geng/Ba Kinn), 82, *126*, 130–131

Meat Sauce over Rice (Lu Rou Fan / Loh Bah Bun), *166*, 180, *181*

Minced, Noodles with Fermented Bean Sauce and (Zha Jiang Mian), 154–155, *155*

in Noodle Soup, Danzai (Dan Zai Mian), 138, *139*

Noodle Soup, Fried Pork Chop, 146–147, *147*

Pig's Knuckle, Red-Braised (Hong Shao Zhu Jiao), 182

Pork Belly, Red-Braised (Hong Shao Rou), 183, *184*

Pot Stickers, Napa Cabbage and, Pan-Fried (Guotie), 73–75, *74*, *75*

Rice, Fried, with Tea Leaves and (Cha Ye Chao Fan), 194–195, *195*

Rice Noodles, Pan-Fried, with Vegetables and (Chao Mi Fen), *152*, 153

Shredded, and Napa Cabbage Stew (Xi Lu Rou), 196, *197*

Slivered, Stir-Fried, with Yellow Chives (Jiu Huang Rou Si), 187

Soup Stock, Basic (Tun Gao Tang), 128

Spareribs, Crispy, Soup with Winter Melon (Pai Gu Su Tang), 150–151

Steamed Ground, with Pickles (Gua Zai Rou), 188

in Sticky Rice, Molded (Tong Zai Mi Gao), 92, 93

Stir-Fry, Hakka-Style (Ke Jia Xiao Chao), *185*, 186

Pot Stickers, Pork and Napa Cabbage, Pan-Fried (Guotie), 73–75, *74*, *75*

Q

Qing Dynasty, 21–22, 23, 27

R

Radish. *See* Daikon Radish

Railroad system, 174

Red-Braised Pig's Knuckle (Hong Shao Zhu Jiao), 182

Red-Braised Pork Belly (Hong Shao Rou), 183, *184*

Religion, 82

Relish, Pickled Mustard Greens (Xue Cai), 60

Rice, 47

Chicken, Shredded, over (Ji Rou Fan), 176

Congee, Sweet Potato (Di Gua Xi Fan), 164, *165*

Fried, Crab (Xie Rou Chao Fan), 227

Fried, with Pork and Tea Leaves (Cha Ye Chao Fan), 194–195, *195*

Pork Meat Sauce over (Lu Rou Fan / Loh Bah Bun), *166*, 180, *181*

Sticky Rice, Molded (Tong Zai Mi Gao), 92, 93

Rice Noodles, *42*, 43

Pan-Fried, with Pork and Vegetables (Chao Mi Fen), *152*, 153

in Soup, Thick, with Pork Meatballs (Rou Geng/Ba Kinn), 82, *126*, 130–131

Soup, Crispy Spareribs, with Winter Melon (Pai Gu Su Tang), 150–151

Soup, Spanish Mackerel (Tu Tun Yu Geng Mian), 145

Rice vinegar, 44

Rice wine, 44

S

Salad, Tomato, with Ginger-Soy Dip (Liang Ban Fan Qie), 100

Sauce(s)

Black Bean, Oysters with (Yin Chi E Zai // Yin Xi O Ah), 214, *215*

Date, Pan-Fried Tofu with (Gan Mei Dou Fu), 120, *121*

Dumpling Dipping (Jiaozi Jiang), 56

Five-Flavor, Steamed Cod with (Wu Wei Yu), 208, *209*

Pork Meat, over Rice (Lu Rou Fan / Loh Bah Bun), *166*, 180, *181*

Sesame, Chilled Noodles with Chicken and (Liang Mian), 157

Sha-Cha (Sha Cha Jiang), 47, 53

Sweet-and-Sour Citrus and Soy-Based (Yang Sheng Zhan Jiang), 55

Sweet-and-Sour Tomato-Based (Hai Shan Jiang), 54

Seafood. *See also* Clam(s); Oyster(s); Shrimp; Shrimp, Dried; Squid

Crab Fried Rice (Xie Rou Chao Fan), 227

with Egg Noodles, Pan-Fried (Hai Xian Chao Mian), 148

Sesame

oil, 47

Oil, Wine-Stewed Chicken with (Ma You Ji), 177, *178*

Sauce, Chilled Noodles with Chicken and (Liang Mian), 157

Thin Noodles, -Scented (Ma You Mian Xian), *156*, 156

Sha-Cha Sauce (Sha Cha Jiang), 47, 53

Sha-Cha Stir-Fried Beef with Watercress, (Sha Cha Niu Rou Kong Xin Cai), *190–191*, 192

Shallots

Fried (Hong Cong Tou), 52

Oysters, Chilled, with Black Vinegar, Cilantro and (Cong Xiag Xian E // Cong Xian Xian Ke), 217

Shiitake Mushrooms, Dried, 43

Cabbage, Braised, with Dried Shrimp and (Lu Bai Cai), 105, *107*

Chicken Soup with Bamboo Shoots and Mushrooms (Zhu Sun Ji Tang), 159

in Pork, Shredded, and Napa Cabbage Stew (Xi Lu Rou), 196, *197*

in Rice Noodles, Pan-Fried, with Pork and Vegetables (Chao Mi Fen), *152*, 153

in Sticky Rice, Molded (Tong Zai Mi Gao), 92, 93

Shin Yeh restaurant, Taiwan, 18

Shrimp

Egg Noodles, Pan-Fried, with Seafood (Hai Xian Chao Mian), 148

in Noodle Soup, Danzai (Dan Zai Mian), 138, *139*

Pan-Fried, with Tea Leaves (Cha Ye Da Xia), 224

Rolls, Deep-Fried (Xia Juan), 225

Wine-Braised (Shao Jiu Xia), 226

Shrimp, Dried, *42*, 43

Cabbage, Braised, with Shiitake Mushrooms and (Lu Bai Cai), 105, *107*

Leek Buns with, Pan-Fried (Jiu Cai Shui Jian Bao), 70–71

Sha-Cha Sauce (Sha Cha Jiang), 47, 53

Snacks. *See* Appetizers/street food snacks

Soup(s). *See also* Noodle Soup(s)

Chicken, with Bamboo Shoots and Mushrooms (Zhu Sun Ji Tang), 159

Chicken, Pineapple and Bitter Melon (Ku Gua Feng Li Ji Tang), 162, *163*

Clam and Daikon Radish (Ge Li Luo Buo Tang), 158

dumplings, 136, *137*

Spareribs, Crispy, with Winter Melon (Pai Gu Su Tang), 150–151

Stock, Basic Pork (Tun Gao Tang), 128

Thick, with Squid (You Yu Geng), 160, *161*

Soy

and Citrus-Based Sauce, Sweet-and-Sour (Yang Sheng Zhan Jiang), 55

-Ginger Dip, Tomato Salad with (Liang Ban Fan Qie), 100, *101*

-Pickled Cucumbers, Sweet (Yan Xiao Huang Gua), 62

sauces, types of, 47

Soybeans. *See* Edamame

Spanish Mackerel Noodle Soup (Tu Tun Yu Geng Mian), 145
Spareribs, Crispy, Soup with Winter Melon (Pai Gu Su Tang), 150–151
Spinach, Water, Sautéed, with Fermented Tofu (Fu Ru Kong Xin Cai), 110, *111*
Squash, Loofah, Clams Braised with (Ge Li Si Gua), 221
Squid
    in Coffin Cake (Guan Cai Ban), 78–79, *79*
    Egg Noodles, Pan-Fried, with Seafood (Hai Xian Chao Mian), 148
    in Pork Stir-Fry, Hakka-Style (Ke Jia Xiao Chao), *185*, 186
    Thick Soup with (You Yu Geng), 160, *161*
    Three Cup (San Bei Xiao Juan), 212, *213*
Stew, Shredded Pork and Napa Cabbage (Xi Lu Rou), 196, *197*
Sticky Rice, Molded (Tong Zai Mi Gao), *92*, 93
Stinky tofu, 123–124, *125*
Stir-Fry(ied)
    Beef with Pickled Mustard Greens and Bean Sprouts (Zha Cai Niu Rou Si), 189
    Beef, Sha-Cha, with Watercress, (Sha Cha Niu Rou Kong Xin Cai), *190–191*, 192
    Pork, Hakka-Style (Ke Jia Xiao Chao), *185*, 186
    Pork, Slivered, with Yellow Chives (Jiu Huang Rou Si), 187
Stock, Basic Pork (Tun Gao Tang), 128
Street food snacks. *See* Appetizers/street food snacks
Sugar, *45*, 47
Sunflower student movement, 15
Sun Yat-sen, 23
Sweet Potato
    Balls, Deep-Fried (You Zha Di Gua Qiu), 117
    Congee (Di Gua Xi Fan), 164, *165*
    Leaves with Garlic, Sautéed (Suan Rong Fan Shu Ye), 109
    Sweet potato leaf metaphor, 19
    Sweet potato starch, 47
Sweet and Sour Glaze, Pan-Fried Pork Liver with (Jian Zhu Gan), 193
Sweet-and-Sour Sauce
    Citrus and Soy-Based (Yang Sheng Zhan Jiang), 55
    Date, Pan-Fried Tofu with (Gan Mei Dou Fu), 120, *121*
    Tomato-Based (Hai Shan Jiang), 54

T
Taipei, *25*, 27, *238–239*
Taipei World Financial Center, 23
Taiwan. *See also* Agriculture; Taiwanese cuisine
    -China trade, 15
    cultural identity in, 15, 18
    democratic development of, 13, 23
    economic growth of, 23
    fishing industry in, 35
    geography and climate of, *32*, 33, *34*, 35, *38–39*
    history of, 21, *22–23*
    immigration from mainland China to, 13, 22, 23, 27, 135–136
    Japanese occupation of, 22–23, 174
    military villages (juan cun), *134–135*, 136–137
    peoples of, 27, 29
    political tensions in, 11–12, 13, 15
    population of, 29
    railroad system in, 174
    religious practice in, 82
Taiwanese cuisine
    bento boxes, *172*, 173–174
    ingredients in, 41, 43, 44, *45*, 47
    and mainland food legacy, 135–137
    in night markets, *80–81*, 81
    obsession with food, 12–13
    stinky tofu, *122–123*, 123–124, *125*
    tea-based, 240
    texture in, 203–204
    traditional, 12, 15, 18–19
Taoism, 82
Tapioca Pearl Tea (Zhen Zhu Nai Cha), *236*, 237
Taro root metaphor, 19
Tarts, Pineapple (Feng Li Su), 230–231, *231*
Tea
    Eggs (Cha Ye Dan), *84*, 85
    leaves, garnishing/braising with, 240
    Leaves, Rice, Fried, with Pork and (Cha Ye Chao Fan), 194–195, *195*
    Leaves, Shrimp with, Pan-Fried (Cha Ye Da Xia), 224
    Sweet Green, Hakka-Style (Ke Jia Lei Cha), *242*, 243
    Tapioca Pearl (Zhen Zhu Nai Cha), *236*, 237
Tea ceremony, 240
Tea growing, *24*, 35, *35*, 239–240, *241*

Tea seed oil, 240
Three Cup Chicken (San Bei Ji), 168, *169*
Three Cup Squid (San Bei Xiao Juan), 212, *213*
Tofu, *122*
    Custard, Sweet (Tian Dou Hua), *248*, 249
    Dry, with Edamame (Dou Gan Chao Mao Dou Ren), *118*, 119
    Fermented, with Sautéed Water Spinach (Fu Ru Kong Xin Cai), 110, *111*
    fermented, stinky tofu (street snack), 123–124, *125*
    Pan-Fried, with Date Sauce (Gan Mei Dou Fu), 120, *121*
Tomato
    -Based Sauce, Sweet-and-Sour (Hai Shan Jiang), 54
    Salad with Ginger-Soy Dip (Liang Ban Fan Qie), 100, *101*
2-2-8 massacre, 23

V
Vegetables. *See also specific vegetables*
    Rice Noodles, Pan-Fried, with Pork and (Chao Mi Fen), *152*, 153
Vinegar-Pickled Cabbage (Suan Cai), *59*, 61

W
Wang Zhi, 124
Watercress, Sha-Cha Stir-Fried Beef with (Sha Cha Niu Rou Kong Xin Cai), *190–191*, 192
Watermelon Shake, Fresh (Xi Gua Bing Sha), 244, *245*
Water Spinach, Sautéed, with Fermented Tofu (Fu Ru Kong Xin Cai), 110, *111*
Wheat noodles, 43, 136
Wine
    Chicken with Sesame Oil, -Stewed (Ma You Ji), 177, *178*
    Clams, -Marinated (Yan Ge Li // Xin Ha Ma), 220, *222*
    Shrimp, -Braised (Shao Jiu Xia), 226

Y
Yam starch, 47
Yellow Chives, Stir-Fried Slivered Pork with (Jiu Huang Rou Si), 187